THE AGE OF ILLUSIONS

The Political Economy of Britain
1968–1982

THE AGE OF ILLUSIONS

The Political Economy of Britain
1968–1982

by

MICHAEL NEVIN

LONDON
VICTOR GOLLANCZ LTD
1983

Dedicated to
the memory of my mother
Winifred Elizabeth Nevin
May 27 1928
July 13 1983

British Library Cataloguing in Publication Data
Nevin, Michael
The age of illusions: the political economy of Britain, 1968–1982.
1. Great Britain – Economic conditions – 1945–
2. Great Britain – Politics and government – 1964–
I. Title
330.94′0858 HC256.6

ISBN 0–575–03331–2
ISBN 0–575–03393–2 Pbk

Printed and bound in Great Britain at
The Camelot Press Ltd, Southampton

Is it possible that nothing important or real has yet been seen or known or said? Is it possible that mankind has had thousands of years in which to observe, reflect, record, and allowed these millennia to slip by like the break at school in which one eats a sandwich and an apple?

Yes, it is possible.

Is it possible that, despite our discoveries and progress . . . we still remain on the surface of life? . . .

Yes, it is possible.

Is it possible that the whole history of the world has been misunderstood? . . .

Yes, it is possible.

Is it possible that these people know with perfect accuracy a past that has never existed? Is it possible that all the realities are nothing to them, that their life runs on, unconnected with anything, like a watch in an empty room?

Yes, it is possible . . .

But if all this is possible – if it has even no more than a semblance of possibility – then surely . . . something must be done.

Rilke, *Malte Laurids Brigge*

ACKNOWLEDGEMENTS

The author thanks the following copyright holders for permission to use material:

The quotation that begins this book, from *The Notebook of Malte Laurids Brigge* by Rilke, is translated by John Linton and used by courtesy of the translator's Literary Estate and The Hogarth Press Ltd. The quotation from *War and Peace* that appears on page 125 is translated by Constance Garnett and used by courtesy of the publisher, William Heinemann Ltd. Passages from *The Future of Socialism* by Anthony Crosland, published by Jonathan Cape Ltd, are used by courtesy of the Estate of C. A. R. Crosland. Other, shorter, quoted passages are acknowledged where they appear and in the Bibliography.

Material taken from the report of the Donovan Commission, *Report on Trade Unions and Employers' Associations, 1965–1968* (1968), from *The Beveridge Report on Social Insurance and Allied Services* (1942), data derived from L.C.E.S., *The British Economy, Key Statistics, 1900–1966* (1971), from various editions of the *Annual Abstract of Statistics*, and from C.S.O., *Economic Trends: Annual Supplement*, 1982 edition, is all reproduced with the permission of the Controller of Her Majesty's Stationery Office.

The figures for British monetary growth were provided by the Bank of England; from 1963 onwards they are consistent with the March 1983 issue of the *Bank of England Quarterly Bulletin*, and for earlier years annual figures are published in a supplement to the September 1969 *Quarterly Bulletin* (pages 372–3).

The source of the Table on page 82 is *The Economics of Inflation* by J. A. Trevithick and C. Malvey, published by Martin Robertson, 1975, that on page 84, the I.M.F. Survey, November 1979, and that on page 179, the I.M.F.'s *International Financial Statistics*, 1982.

CONTENTS

PREFACE

IN JULY OF 1979 I was coming to the end of a two-year contract with the Government of St Lucia in the West Indies. Conscious of the fact that I ought to start looking for another job, I asked the island's Prime Minister, John Compton, to write me a reference for an application to the World Bank in Washington. This request had met with no response, for there was a move afoot to keep me on as an economist in St Lucia; and the fear was that if my application to the World Bank was successful, the attractions of a highly-paid job in the United States would tempt me away from the Caribbean.

But in St Lucia itself, a General Election was due. There was a feeling of change in the air: an expectation that John Compton, after fifteen years in power, faced defeat for the first time in his political career.

Less than a week before the General Election, I got a phone-call from Compton asking me to come to his office. When I reached it, I found him sitting there alone, surrounded by a mass of official papers, still working in the deserted government buildings. He told me that he was going to write me a reference for the World Bank, and for about half an hour we discussed what should go into it. As I prepared to leave, I asked him what he planned to do after the Election.

There was a pause. Finally, he looked towards me with an enigmatic gaze, and said,

"After? Then we need to get back to work. The civil servants' strike has put the country back three months. We have to make up for lost time."

Suddenly I felt a shock of terrible poignancy. For at that moment I realised that Compton knew he was going to lose the election. He was writing me a reference now because he would not be in a position to ask me to stay on after the election. And I was curiously moved that in the middle of a hard campaign, he had taken the time to lend a helping hand to a junior member of the Civil Service. In the tumult of a confused world, a personal kindness is never forgotten.

Six days later, Compton's United Workers' Party went down to defeat in the St Lucian general election. Some three weeks afterwards, I was having a dinner party for a few close friends in my apartment at Vigie Bay. I ran out of drinks, and late in the evening drove down to Castries, the capital of St Lucia, to buy some more bottles from a local rumshop. There was an atmosphere of tension in the town; hundreds of people were roaming the streets; windows were being smashed and shops looted. I had walked into the middle of a riot, which had erupted, provoked by the new government, when the leaders of the United Workers' Party had tried to rally their supporters in their first public meeting since the election.

Two months later, I was back in Britain and out of a job. Despite the reference of the former Prime Minister of St Lucia, my application to the World Bank had been rejected. The sunswept beaches of the Caribbean seemed a universe away as I queued up for supplementary benefit at the onset of a freezing British winter. I had no more prospect of getting a job than anyone else among the mounting ranks of the unemployed. If I had seen with my own eyes the beginnings of the decline of the tiny economy of St Lucia on the night of the Castries riot, I was now the victim of the decline of the British economy, less dramatic but ultimately more devastating than what was happening in St Lucia. In both nations general elections in 1979 had brought to power governments more interested in the pursuit of a political dogma than in the welfare of the common people. In both nations it was ordinary people who became the victims of the consequences of that pursuit: the erosion of productive capacity and jobs as new investment dried up and existing assets were liquidated.

It was to be three months before I found another job. During that period, I bought myself a typewriter out of my rapidly dwindling savings, and began this book. I was determined to piece together the complex jigsaw that pictured the inexorable decline of the British economy since 1968. I felt that if only a clear analysis of what had gone wrong could be developed, it would contain within it the germs of a solution to the manifold problems which pressed down on Britain as the 1980s began.

It was already clear that the liberal conventional wisdom of the 1950s and 1960s had run out of ideas. Instead of developing new tools of analysis, shaped to tackle the problems of the 1970s, it had gone up the blind alley of piecemeal institutional reform and intervention in the labour market.

All the running in the intellectual world was being made by the new Right, by social scientists like Friedman and Hayek. Whatever else may be said of them, their writings at least had the advantage of being lucid, simple, and decisive, in contrast to the growing muddle of liberal thinking. At the British General Election in 1979, the new orthodoxy of the monetarist Right scored a clear political victory, and the Conservative Party under Margaret Thatcher gained power.

But during the succeeding three years while I was writing the book, between 1979 and 1982, it became increasingly evident that monetarism did not offer the solution to Britain's economic decline. Unemployment rose dramatically, doubling between 1979 and 1982 to more than three million; while national income contracted by almost 5 per cent in real terms, with the brunt of the decline being borne by the manufacturing sector, whose production fell by a sixth.

The events in Britain lent increasing conviction to my thesis, and to the strategy for recovery developed from it. I have tried to spell out this thesis in a clear and non-technical manner. The only section which the intelligent layman may find difficult is that on monetary policy, in the third part of Chapter Three; and this section may be skipped without destroying the flow of the argument.

There is no doubt that the strategy advocated in the concluding sections of this book can be implemented. There are those who claim that there is no alternative to the particular brand of monetarism pursued by the Thatcher Government; but this is patent nonsense. The possibility for change always exists.

In St Lucia, after three years of suffering a government concerned more with political theology than with the real world, the electorate decisively switched its allegiance and returned Compton's United Workers' Party to office by a landslide in mid-1982. A start has since been made in reversing the decline of the 1979–82 era, and generating new investment and jobs, to enrich an economy far poorer than that of Britain.

What is true of St Lucia is also true of Britain, and indeed of all human affairs. Most of the problems that men face have been created by men themselves. And if men create their own problems, then they can also resolve them. There is no inevitability about the state in which the world, or any nation or individual within it, finds itself. There is always an alternative.

LUXEMBOURG, APRIL 1983 MICHAEL NEVIN

Chapter One

THE FOUNDATIONS OF CONSENSUS

> The redeeming feature of war is that it puts a nation to the test. As exposure to the atmosphere reduces all mummies to instant dissolution, so war passes supreme judgement on social systems that have outlived their usefulness.
>
> Karl Marx, *The Eastern Question*

I

ON SUNDAY February 13th, 1977, the British Foreign Secretary, Anthony Crosland, drove to the village of Deddington to buy the Sunday newspapers, and afterwards went for a brief walk. When he got back home, he resumed work on his official papers. Shortly afterwards he stopped, and said to his wife Susan, with a note of anxiety in his voice,

"Something has happened."

It was a stroke. His wife drove him to the Radcliffe Infirmary in Oxford, where his condition steadily deteriorated. He died the following Saturday, February 19th.

The tributes to the dead Foreign Secretary in the British House of Commons were led by the Prime Minister, James Callaghan. He recalled the early days of the post-war era.

"We were both delegates to the Council of Europe at Strasbourg, and we watched, as young men, the great figures of Europe, occasionally being allowed to join in. There was one historic day when we watched the German delegates march into the chamber for the first time. It was a great day of reconciliation which I think those of us present will not forget."

But by February of 1977 the optimism of these early days had evaporated. The guiding ideas of the first quarter century after World War Two no longer seemed capable of tackling the problems facing Britain in the 1970s. Anthony Crosland had developed these ideas more clearly and comprehensively than any other British politician in his major theoretical work *The Future of Socialism*, published in the mid-1950s. Of this book, the leader of the Liberal Party, David Steel, said in his tribute to Crosland:

"Looking back over the last twenty years, it is difficult to think of any work which has had a comparable impact on a whole generation of people interested about the future of the country."

The death of Anthony Crosland marks the final passing of the era of consensus. A consensus Prime Minister, James Callaghan, struggled on in office for another two years, at the head of a government with no coherent programme, much of its time taken up with a desperate fight for survival. But the other major figures of the consensus era had faded from the scene: Gaitskell was dead; Macmillan and R. A. Butler had both long since retired; Edward Heath had been defeated as leader of the Conservative Party in 1975; Maudling was discredited; Wilson had resigned as Prime Minister in 1976; and shortly afterwards, Roy Jenkins had departed from British politics to become President of the European Commission in Brussels.

The unprecedented economic growth and high level of employment which formed the basis of the consensus had given way in the 'seventies to accelerating inflation, a rising level of unemployment, and negligible real growth. The generation which had grown to maturity in the 1950s and 1960s were by now middle-aged, and clung on to their jobs and security. The real victims of the hard times were the new generation, uncertain of what the future held for them. The harsher economic climate which faced them was reflected in a less confident attitude in youth, as the easygoing lifestyle and music of the 'sixties gave way to a raw hopelessness.

What has gone wrong, and why? How, if at all, can the problems be overcome and affluence and full employment restored?

This book will start its examination of these questions by going back to the beginning, to the foundations of consensus.

II

Viewed in retrospect, the quarter century after the end of the Second World War seems like a Golden Age. The years of conflict were succeeded by a generation which enjoyed the fruits of peace. And it was a peace with prosperity, after the waste and hardships of the Depression years before the Second World War. It was also a peace which saw the flowering of democracy in Western Europe, which grew from the ashes of the most fearsome and evil tyranny the world has ever known.

It may seem paradoxical to say that without the Second World War there would have been no Golden Age. But nevertheless this is almost certainly the case. In Britain, the war transformed the machinery of government and attitudes to its use. It laid the basis for the Welfare State. It precipitated the introduction of Keynesian techniques for the management of the economy. And finally, the unity of the nation in victory gave rise to the bipartisan approach to foreign policy adopted after 1945. It was on this tripod, of the Welfare State, Keynesian economics, and a bipartisan foreign policy, that the era of consensus was founded.

It was the Second World War which stimulated the creation of the Welfare State in Britain, and marked the culmination of a process which had been going on since the Industrial Revolution in the eighteenth century. This was the process whereby the needs of the State to mobilise effectively for war had caused a progressive widening of the social services it provided to its potential soldiers.

In a largely forgotten book published in 1954, one writer, Andrzewjewski, elevated to the status of a general theory the dictum of the nineteenth-century German sociologist Max Weber, that "the discipline of the army gives birth to all discipline".

Andrzewjewski argued that the military participation ratio: that is, the proportion of the total population actively engaged in the execution of war: determines the social stratification of a society. His thesis was that, as a society progresses technologically, the proportion of its people who will be drawn into its wars increases. As it increases, the division between those who fight wars and the remainder of the population erodes. In a pre-industrial society, wars affect only a small part of the population; and the war effort is organised and controlled by a few military leaders recruited from a social élite, whose power depends on the backing of only a tiny proportion of the total population. Consequently the ruling élite has no need for the active support of a war from the ordinary population. With the advent of industrialisation, however, different sectors of the economy become more highly integrated and the scope of war is extended. The more highly integrated the production process becomes, the greater the ability of any particular group in society to disrupt the war effort. So the ruling élite becomes increasingly concerned about securing the active support of the entire population; and this requires that the spoils of victory are distributed more equitably than in a pre-industrial society.

Thus, in Britain, the ruling élite first became concerned with the quantity of men of fighting age during the Industrial Revolution. The British Government instituted its first Population Census at the time of the Napoleonic Wars in 1801, and this established authoritatively the number of potential soldiers in the population.

The next advance occurred at the time of the Crimean War in the mid-nineteenth century, when concern with the quality of treatment for injured soldiers resulted in the improvements in nursing and military hospitals associated with Florence Nightingale.

The Boer War at the end of the nineteenth century generated a concern with the quality of all recruits, and not merely enlisted soldiers, because most of the volunteers for the war in South Africa had to be rejected on the grounds of unfitness. The experience of the Boer War gave clear evidence that, to recruit a physically fit standing army in time of war, it was necessary to ensure the health not merely of the men recruited, but also of potential recruits in the population, including male children who were the next generation of recruits. In the years after the Boer War, local authorities were empowered to provide free school meals for needy children; and school medical inspection was introduced. These acts were followed by the 1911 Insurance Act, which constituted the single most important attempt to improve the calibre of the potential army during the Edwardian period. The 1911 Act introduced comprehensive insurance for male workers against sickness and unemployment on a basis of contributions of 4d. from each employee, 3d. from the employer, and 2d. from the government, for each insured employee. Thus, the effective cover a worker would get was worth "9d. for 4d.", on which slogan the scheme was sold.

Yet these reforms did not tackle the fundamental cause of the low level of fitness and health among the working population, which was poverty. The measures attacked the underlying problem of poverty only indirectly, by helping the children of poor families, and providing limited insurance for men in work, rather than by alleviating the poverty of families where the male head was out of work, or earning an income insufficient to meet the family's needs. The consequence was that Britain entered the First World War a malnourished and unfit nation.

To induce men to fight, the Government had to offer them

something more afterwards than a return to a constant struggle for mere physical subsistence. This they did: the prospect talked of as the fruit of victory was a "land fit for heroes to live in". But the nature of the post-war General Election, engineered by Lloyd George to maintain his personal position as Prime Minister, ensured the return of a right-wing Government representing the interests of the better-off sections of the population, and unsympathetic to any further extension of the social services. The only concession made to the returning troops – largely in the fear that if it was not made there would be a violent backlash – was the introduction of the dole, a payment to unemployed former soldiers who were not covered by national insurance and had no other form of income. Some years later, in 1925, Neville Chamberlain's Widows, Orphans and Old Age Contributory Pensions Act integrated dependants into the insurance system instituted in 1911, and thus provided a minimum assurance that the death of a British soldier in a future war would not leave his wife, children or aged parents utterly destitute.

The advent of Blitzkrieg in World War Two forced the Government to make further concessions. No longer would the distribution of a few crumbs to soldiers and their dependants be sufficient. The conduct of war by air blurred the distinction between the military and non-military population for ever. Not only were the efforts of the civilian population essential to the execution of the war, but civilians were now also potential casualties. Altogether, some 60,000 British civilians were killed in air-raids in World War Two, of whom 20,000 died in London during the Blitz. Since the war-effort depended on the whole population, the State had to take steps to maintain not only their physical health, but also their morale, or psychological commitment to the war. This necessitated a social policy that was both comprehensive and just.

The blueprint for such a policy was set out in the Beveridge Report of 1942. Beveridge saw five "Giants" standing in the way of the "Road to Reconstruction" which would have to be tackled after the war. These giants were Want, associated with low family income relative to the size of the family; Disease, caused by malnutrition and inadequate medical services; Squalor, deriving from poor housing; Ignorance, arising from lack of education; and Idleness, or unemployment, the scourge of the inter-war years. Of these five related problems, Beveridge was primarily concerned with Want, and the White Paper on Social Insurance presented in 1944 on the basis of his proposals articulated the new attitude of Government.

> The [social insurance] scheme as a whole will embrace, not certain occupations and income-groups, but the entire population. Concrete expression is thus given to the solidarity and unity of the nation, which in war have been bulwarks against aggression and in peace will be its guarantees of success in the fight against individual want and mischance.

The Beveridge Report laid down the principles by which this fight would be carried out.

Firstly, it proposed that the existing structure of social services should be built on, rather than torn down and replaced by a completely new framework. By implication, this meant acceptance of the insurance principle embodied in the 1911 Act. Benefits would be paid out of a fund into which potential beneficiaries were expected to make regular contributions when they were employed. An alternative socialist solution, which would have provided everyone in need directly from taxation revenue, was rejected. Indeed, so far from the system subsequently developed causing a redistribution of income from rich taxpayers to poor beneficiaries, it was calculated in 1949 that the working class (defined as those with incomes of £500 p.a. or less) paid in taxes £139 million more than they received in benefits from the social services.

The second principle enunciated by Beveridge was that the social insurance system should be universal, embracing every member of society. Previously, the beneficiaries of the social services in Britain had been the military or the potential military; or those regarded as too inadequate to look after themselves. The adoption of the principle of universality eliminated the mark of shame on a civilian applying for State benefits. Now that every citizen had the right to claim them, the benefits were no longer regarded as charity for the destitute.

The third major principle of the Beveridge Report was that the level of insurance provided should permit no more than mere subsistence. A minimum income was guaranteed to all of the nation's citizens, but no more, because it was not intended that the universal social insurance system should create a disincentive to work.

In sum, what Beveridge proposed was a consolidation and rationalisation of the existing structure, rather than a radically new departure. And in fact, this process of consolidation and rationalisation had begun before Beveridge produced his Report. It had been stimulated by the exigencies of the war.

The first giant, Want, was already being overcome by the development of national insurance, which was extended in the course of the Second World War. Although universal family allowances were not introduced until 1945, dependants' allowances for the wives and children of servicemen were introduced early in the war. More importantly, the Goverment encouraged the adoption of a more nutritious diet, particularly by mothers and their young children. Five days after the Dunkirk evacuation began in May 1940, the Government began to subsidise milk. The price of milk fell from 4½d. to 2d. a pint, and about a third of all mothers with young children received their milk free of charge. In addition, the distribution of milk through the state educational system was extended, and by the end of the war about three-quarters of all schoolchildren took school milk. School meals were also subsidised, and the proportion of those taking school meals increased from one-thirtieth of the school population before the war, to one-third by the end of it.

The measures to alleviate Want also reduced the incidence of Disease. Despite the fact that in total there was less food to go round, nutritional standards actually improved in Britain during the war, because of the more equitable distribution of resources through the rationing system, particularly of such home-produced essentials as bread, cheese, meat, vegetables and fresh fruit.

As well as improvements in diet, which helped to prevent diseases, there were improvements in curative health treatment under the impact of war. In the 1930s hospital services in Britain left much to be desired. Voluntary hospitals co-existed with local authority hospitals which were frequently prison-like in their design and obsolete in their equipment. The lack of overall co-ordination between these two systems gave rise to serious mis-allocations between hospitals – not only of physical facilities, but also of doctors, consultants, and nursing staff. The consequence was long waiting lists for hospital treatment. In 1938 an estimated 100,000 people were waiting to enter local authority hospitals. However, after the Munich Agreement the Government took action to integrate all hospitals into a general system in anticipation of war. The Government's original intention had been to maintain the existing unintegrated system for the civilian population, and to develop a national system based on regional groups of hospitals for war casualties. But in practice it was difficult to maintain the dividing-line between the two systems, and a single system was gradually set up.

The elimination of Ignorance, the third giant, was continued through the 1944 Education Act. Like action against Want, it was based on liberal rather than socialist principles. Its objective was to offer equality of opportunity to schoolchildren within the State system, rather than egalitarianism. Private education, which offered privileges and opportunities unavailable to children in State schools, was left untouched.

The 1944 Act instituted a division in the State sector between primary education up to the age of eleven, and secondary education which was initially compulsory to the age of fourteen, and raised to fifteen in 1947. At primary level children were taught basic literacy and numeracy. Secondary education was divided between grammar, secondary modern, and technical schools, the allocation to which was determined by the results of a competitive examination, the "eleven-plus", taken by schoolchildren at the end of their primary education. Those successful in the eleven-plus went to grammar school, where they were taught academic subjects, leading ultimately to university for the most able. Those children who were unsuccessful in the eleven-plus went to technical or secondary modern schools, where they learnt practical subjects which were intended to lay the basis for a trade when they left school. Each of the three types of school had in theory a "parity of esteem" with the others; but, in practice, the grammar schools soon gained pre-eminence. The Government spent most money per pupil on grammar schools, and the children going to grammar schools had far better job prospects than did those going to technical or secondary modern schools.

Little action was taken against Squalor, the fourth of Beveridge's giants, during the war years. However, legislation which would give a peacetime Government the muscle to deal with it was passed in the form of the 1944 Town and Country Planning Act. This Act increased the powers of compulsory purchase by Government in blitzed, slum and overcrowded areas.

Finally, the impact of war eliminated Idleness. All available manpower was drawn into employment and conscription of women started in 1941 in an effort to maximise output. The rate of unemployment, which had averaged 16 per cent of the working population in the decade 1930–39, was reduced to 6½ per cent in 1940, 2½ per cent in 1941, and less than 1 per cent in 1942 and 1943.

The social reforms introduced in World War Two and the blueprint for post-war reconstruction outlined in the Beveridge Report mark the culmination of the process analysed by Andrzewjewski. As the proportion of the British population actively involved in the execution of war had increased in the century and a half following the Industrial Revolution, so British Governments had become successively concerned with the quantity of potential soldiers (during the Napoleonic Wars), the medical treatment of soldiers (during the Crimean War), the physical fitness of all potential recruits (during the Boer War), the psychological commitment or morale of soldiers and their dependants (during the First World War), and finally the morale, physical fitness and economic security of the whole population (during the Second World War).

During the period of the Second World War, despite all the hardships, the nutrition of the population of Britain actually improved. The material standard of life overall fell, as the nation's resources were consumed in the war effort, but for the very poor and those who had comprised the long-term unemployed at the outbreak of war living standards increased. The message of the war years was clear – central planning could work, and the provision of social services by Government could benefit many poor people at an acceptable cost.

The choice which faced the voters in 1945 at the General Election following victory in Europe was either a consolidation and extension of the planning machinery and social services developed during the war, as was advocated by the party of the left, the Labour Party; or a reduction in Government intervention in the economy, as was desired by most of the Conservative Party.

The Conservatives felt that government intervention on the scale of the war years was incompatible with individual freedom in peacetime. However, they had been in power continuously, either alone or in coalition, ever since 1916, except for two brief periods of Labour minority government in 1923 and 1929–31. They were consequently identified with the failures of the inter-war years –

with mass unemployment at home and the appeasement of Hitler and Mussolini abroad.

The electorate voted decisively for the Labour Party, which was returned to office with a majority of more than 150 seats in the 630-seat House of Commons. The new Labour Government proceeded to build on the reforms of the war years, and to establish a Welfare State, which ensured for every citizen "from the cradle to the grave" a minimum income which would be enough to live on.

The giant of Want, which had been accepted as inevitable by the politicians who had governed Britain before the Second World War, was overcome by a series of statutes passed in the years 1945 to 1948. The 1945 Family Allowances Act introduced a universal child allowance for the second and subsequent children of a family, financed by the central exchequer. By 1949, nearly five million family allowances were being paid to some three million families in Britain. The Industrial Injuries Act provided comprehensive coverage against accidents at work. The 1946 National Insurance Act, based on the Beveridge principle of flat-rate benefits in return for flat-rate contributions, completed the work begun by the 1911 Act by instituting comprehensive insurance for employees and their dependants against sickness, unemployment, old age and death. For those who had not been in employment long enough to make the minimum required number of contributions to the insurance fund, the 1948 National Assistance Act provided a minimum subsistence income.

With the passing of the National Assistance Act the framework of an integrated social security system was completed. Primary poverty, a condition in which one in every five of the working population had existed only half a century before, was virtually eliminated in Britain. And it was eliminated by means of the Beveridge principle of insurance, without any major redistribution of income from rich to poor. The major redistribution took place within the life-cycle of individual men and women. An individual paid into the insurance scheme when he earned more than enough to cover his immediate requirements – during the phase of his life when he was working but without family responsibilities. He derived benefits from national insurance during the phases of his life when his needs were greater than his earning power – in childhood; when raising a family; and finally when old and retired.

It has been argued that the insurance principle has been

undermined by inflation since the Second World War, because inflation causes the real value of any nominal money contribution to an insurance fund to decline. This is true only if money contributions are left idle in the form of cash; if they are invested by the insurance fund's managers and earn a return at least equal to the rate of inflation, then the real value of contributions does not fall, and may indeed be increasing.

Nor has the growth of earnings-related benefits for an increasing number of workers negated the universality of the social security system. There is still a universal minimum income guaranteed for everyone. The three central principles of the Beveridge Report – the principle of insurance, that benefits should be paid for by contributions; the principle of universality, that the whole population should be covered; and the principle of subsistence, that the coverage should provide only a minimum income, so insurance payments will not constitute a disincentive to work – remain the foundation of the social security system in Britain forty years after the first appearance of the Beveridge Report.

The Beveridge principle that the social services should be self-financing was, however, relaxed in the areas of health and housing. In housing, there was a radical shift in emphasis compared to the inter-war years. The housing policy of the inter-war years, established by Neville Chamberlain when he was Minister of Housing, was founded on the "filter down" theory. The basic approach had been to offer incentives to the private sector to help mainly middle-class house buyers, so that when they left their old homes, those homes would "filter down" to the working class. In this way, it was hoped that the whole population would benefit from improved housing.

The housing boom of the 1930s did indeed result in an overall improvement in housing standards. But the improvement mainly benefited the middle-class home owners, who had been the most comfortable before the boom had started. As far as the working class was concerned, living for the most part in rented accommodation, Squalor remained an unconquered problem in 1939.

By contrast, the policy of the post-war Labour Government was to direct resources to those most in need by concentrating on housing provided by local authorities and maintaining controls over rents in the private sector so that it would not bid away limited resources. Local authority housing was allocated on the basis of need as low rents subsidised by the central exchequer. The thrust in local authority housing increased the number of council houses built in the United Kingdom from 21,000 in 1946 to a peak of 170,000 in 1948. The total then levelled out at 140,000 per annum in 1949–51.

The rents paid by the occupants of council houses covered a part at least of the cost of building and maintaining the houses. In the case of the health service, however, the principle that the beneficiary of the service should pay for it was almost entirely abandoned.

The creation of the National Health Service is remembered today as the achievement of Aneurin Bevan, the leading left-wing figure in the post-war Labour Government. The Service commenced operations in 1948, despite strong opposition from the medical establishment, the Conservative Party, and even some permanent civil servants within Bevan's own Ministry of Health. It was driven through by the personal determination of Aneurin Bevan and became the one part of the structure of the Welfare State based on socialist rather than liberal principles.

Administratively, the National Health Service comprised three distinct elements. The first was the hospital network, which was brought under the auspices of the Ministry of Health and run through twenty Regional Hospital Boards – developing the system set up in wartime. The second element was medical care outside hospitals, which was provided by qualified doctors, dentists, and opticians, practising as individuals or in partnership, and contracting their services to the National Health Service. The third element of the Service was preventative health care, which was provided through Health Centres which were maintained by local authorities.

The operation of the National Health Service cost the exchequer £400 million in its first year, of which 90 per cent was financed from taxation. Since the National Health Service mainly benefited the poor, while the burden of direct taxation fell mainly on the well-off, the introduction of the Service did have a redistributive effect. The National Health Service has ever since been operated on the principle of to those according to their needs, from those (through the taxation system) according to their means.

It was the decision of the Chancellor of the Exchequer, Hugh Gaitskell, to attempt to put the N.H.S. on a partially self-financing basis by introducing a charge on false teeth and spectacles in the

1951 Budget which provoked the resignation from the Government of Bevan and two junior ministers, Harold Wilson and John Freeman. The point at issue was a minor one: the expected revenue from the charges was only some £25 million. But it represented a philosophical split, a shift from a socialist to a liberal basis of financing the National Health Service. As such, the question of National Health Service charges became the focal point of the divisions which were developing in the Labour Party.

By the end of 1948, the Labour Party's basic programme of reform was completed. The framework of the Welfare State and the mixed economy had been established. The Bevanite wing of the party wished to push on, and introduce legislation to enable the State to take over the "commanding heights" of the economy from the private sector and establish a planned economy. But the Bevanites constituted a minority in the Cabinet and the Parliamentary Party, and indeed in the trade union movement outside Parliament. The majority of the Parliamentary Labour Party opted for consolidation. At the 1950 General Election, the Labour Party's Parliamentary majority was reduced to 17 seats. It was in early 1951 that a frustrated Bevan finally resigned from the Government over the issue of National Health Service charges, to campaign for his policies from the backbenches.

While the splits in the Labour Government were widening, the Conservative opposition was preparing itself for a return to office. The Conservative Party has been in office for fifty of the eighty years of the twentieth century so far; and the reason for its predominance has been its ability to adapt to new circumstances, and absorb innovations in the operation of Government. Nowhere did this ability to adapt reveal itself more clearly than in the immediate post-war era.

The party recovered from the shock of being on the wrong end of an electoral landslide in 1945 and set up a Policy Centre and Research Department to develop Conservative philosophy for the post-war era. Some of the ablest young men of the generation were recruited to its staff, including such future political leaders as Iain Macleod, Reginald Maudling and Enoch Powell. The most important landmark in the road back for the Conservatives was passed in 1947, when the Policy Centre's Industrial Policy Committee produced the Industrial Charter which was to lay the basis for future Tory economic and social policy. The Charter accepted full employment and the Welfare State as worthwhile ends of government. It recognised that central government intervention on a much greater scale than during the inter-war period was a necessary means to those ends. But it argued that central government planning should adapt to the needs of the private sector, rather than vice-versa. The Charter therefore advocated that private enterprise should be freed from the constraints placed upon it by physical controls and high taxation.

At the General Election of 1951 the Conservative Party, united on the principles of the Industrial Charter, gained a narrow victory over the divided Labour Party. The new Conservative Government dismantled the physical controls which had been built up over the past decade. Food subsidies and rationing were ended. Controls on private sector housing were done away with. The programme of local authority housebuilding was gradually wound down, and the emphasis was shifted back to the private sector. The number of houses built privately each year, which had averaged only about 30,000 in the late 1940s, increased to well over 100,000 by the late 1950s.

Nevertheless, social security, State education, and the National Health Service were operated under the Conservative Government very much as they had been under its predecessor.

Having rolled back physical controls in the few areas where they had encroached on the allocation of productive resources, the Conservative Government was content to preside over a form of managed capitalism. The allocation of resources was determined largely by the forces of supply and demand in the market; but the provision of universal education, social security, and health treatment by the State ensured a more efficient and a more humane form of capitalism than had existed during the inter-war period.

III

In the generation between the mid-1930s and mid-1950s, there was a quantum leap in the quality of life in Britain, particularly the quality of life enjoyed by the poorer sections of society. Britain led the western world in the provision of cheap rented housing, free health services, and univeral secondary education; and the people who benefited most from them were those who earned too little to buy them on the open market.

Yet the advances in the social services were only made possible by the underlying growth of the economy. Neither the social services nor residential housing contributes directly to the production of goods. Consequently, their extension requires that a surplus of production is generated over the immediate physical needs of the population. The advances in the social services after 1940 were therefore only made possible by a transformation in the way the economy operated.

The most important factor in this transformation was the elimination of mass unemployment. Nearly one-fifth of the working population had been unemployed for much of the 1930s. Within this aggregate, certain areas which depended on the traditional heavy industries of shipbuilding, coal and iron and steel were particularly hard hit. In towns like Merthyr in South Wales and Jarrow on Tyneside most of the adult population was unemployed. Unemployment constituted a waste of productive potential. It meant that goods and services which could have been produced were not, because the men who could have produced them were not usefully employed. More than that, unemployment degraded the men and women it affected. Without a job, a man could not earn an income to feed and clothe his family, and was reduced to being an unwanted and useless burden on society.

With the mobilisation of resources for war, those who had been unemployed throughout the 1930s were given the opportunity to work, in many cases for the first time in their lives. The pitifully inadequate policies against unemployment in the 1930s were shaken by the need for national survival in wartime. A new approach to the management of the national finances was forced upon the Government, an approach which derived from the theories of the most influential western economist of the twentieth century, John Maynard Keynes.

Before Keynes, the Government had managed its finances on very much the same principles as an accountant or company secretary manages the finances of a private company. The first imperative was that revenue should cover expenditure on the current account, and a surplus earned on the current financial year's activities. Debt might be incurred to finance investment expenditure, whose returns would accrue in the future. But debt had to be repaid. So in normal times, some effort should be made to reduce the burden of the National Debt by redeeming part of it from the surplus earned on the current account.

Government expenditure was undertaken on the provision of

public services. These were services not adequately provided for by the open market, because they benefited citizens collectively – that is, no single individual's return from such services was independent of the benefit derived by others. They included defence, internal policing, and primary education.

The amount of Government expenditure on these services was constrained by its revenues from taxes. Government, it was believed, could not spend more than it earned for any length of time. The National Debt could not be increased indefinitely without threatening the collapse of the monetary system. Nor could Government increase its revenue at will, so its expenditure had to be kept under tight rein.

The reason why the Government did not have limitless control over its revenue was because it was believed that the public's tolerance of taxation was severely constrained. Any Government which substantially increased the rate of taxation levied on the populace would risk being thrown out of office by them at the next election.

This approach to the management of the national finances, having as its objectives a balanced budget at as low a level of taxation as possible, and as the means to these ends the tight control of public expenditure through the limitation of government activities to those functions which could not be carried out by the free market, was implemented with greatest success by William Gladstone when he was Chancellor of the Exchequer and Prime Minister in the latter half of the nineteenth century. However, the British economy was knocked out of its nineteenth-century equilibrium by the First World War. It never really recovered during the inter-war years. During the 1920s, unemployment in Britain averaged well over one in ten of the labour force. Yet still the tenets of Gladstonian finance were held sacred by the Treasury civil servants, although alternative views about how the economy should be managed were emerging. The view that unemployment could be reduced by increasing expenditure on public works was advocated by the Liberal Party at the 1929 General Election. John Maynard Keynes published a pamphlet jointly written with the Oxford economist Hubert Henderson entitled *Can Lloyd George Do It?* in which he lent his support to greater public expenditure as a means of creating jobs.

However, the Liberal Party was politically a spent force, and in the 1929 election came a poor third behind the Labour and Conservative Parties. Without a political vehicle to implement them, Keynes' ideas were ignored. Indeed, the intellectual case for them remained to be demonstrated; by the end of the 1920s, Keynes had yet to think through his theories fully.

In June, 1931, one of Keynes' students at Cambridge, Richard Kahn, published a seminal paper on the theory of the multiplier. Keynes himself was becoming more confident of the correctness of the policies he was advocating, and more vigorous in his attack on the Treasury orthodoxy. In *The Means to Prosperity* Keynes wrote:

> It is a complete mistake to believe that there is a dilemma between schemes for increasing employment and schemes for balancing the Budget . . . Quite the contrary. There is no possibility of balancing the Budget except by increasing the national income, which is much the same as increasing employment.

This was a paradoxical statement. What Keynes was saying was that policies to increase employment, such as increased Government spending on public works, were necessary in conditions of economic depression to bring about a balanced budget. The paradox arose because it was totally contrary to the Treasury orthodoxy to suppose that higher spending could improve the financial position of Government, any more than it would improve the financial position of a private business enterprise. According to the conventional wisdom, the reverse would be true.

Keynes' argument rested on the key insight on which his whole theory was based. His essential thesis was that the amount a Government gets in revenue from the taxpayers is not independent of the amount it spends in an economy in which productive resources are not fully employed.

The various strands in Keynes' reasoning were pulled together in his major theoretical work, *The General Theory of Employment, Interest and Money*, published in 1936. The following year, he wrote an article in the *Quarterly Journal of Economics* in which he stated what he saw as the most important theoretical innovation of the General Theory. It was the concept of the consumption function – the notion that current spending, or consumption, is a function of income.

The more a man earns, the more he is likely to spend – this was hardly a revolutionary insight. But if the same principle applies in aggregate: the more an economy earns, the more it spends and vice-versa: then, a sudden slump in income as a result of events external to the economy – as occurred in Britain in 1929–31 – would cause aggregate spending to fall. The fall in spending would reduce the overall value of goods and services that companies could sell. Faced with a fall in their sales revenue, companies would attempt to cut back their expenditure, including their wage-bill. If workers accepted cuts in wages, the reduction in the wage-bill could be achieved without cutting back the number of jobs; if they did not, reducing the wage-bill would imply a reduction in the numbers employed. Either way, the aggregate reduction in wages and other incomes would result in a further fall in consumer spending. And so the downswing in economic activity would be self-perpetuating.

If Government reacted to the initial shock of a fall in national income by trying to cut its own expenditure then it would merely make the situation worse. The reduction in Government expenditure, by fuelling the cumulative fall in National Income, would reduce taxation revenue (which was a function of National Income), and could consequently worsen the Government's budgetary position rather than improve it. Conversely, if Government increased its expenditure, it would increase or at least arrest the decline of National Income. If Government's extra spending gave jobs to more men, the expenditure of the newly employed would increase aggregate demand and draw others into employment, and so on. This was Keynes' essential argument in favour of greater public expenditure.

But in the inter-war years, Keynes on economic policy held a position exactly analogous to Winston Churchill on foreign policy – he was a voice crying in the wilderness. Had it not been for the advent of the Second World War, that is what they both would have remained. Britain's declaration of war against Germany on September 3rd, 1939, dramatically changed the situation. The British Government was faced with the immediate task of putting the economy on a war footing. And here Keynes' approach was of immediate relevance. The economy in wartime had to be viewed as a whole, with Government playing a central role within it, rather than just plugging the worst gaps left by the private sector.

In a series of articles published in *The Times* newspaper in 1940, entitled "How to Pay for the War", Keynes outlined his approach for Government's management of the war economy. He proposed that, rather than assess revenue according to what the taxpayer would bear, and meeting any deficit for military expenditure by borrowing, attention should be paid first to the potential capacity of a fully employed war economy, and then some rational assessment should be made as to how this capacity could best be distributed between war and non-war needs. Essentially, the Keynesian approach was based on two equations. On the supply side of the economy, the quantity of goods and services available for private consumption could not exceed the total capacity of the economy less that amount of total capacity required by the Government for the war effort. On the demand side, the amount of money individuals had for spending on goods and services would be equal to National Income less the proportion of it either saved or taken in taxes.

If money demand exceeded the physical volume of goods and services available for consumption, then inflation would be generated: the price of goods and services would be pulled up and the real value of money demand reduced. This is what had happened in the First World War, when the price-level in Britain had more than doubled. Keynes argued that inflation would occur again in the Second World War if the Government chose to finance military expenditure by printing money, as it had in the First World War. Instead, Keynes advocated that the Government should act on private consumption and taxation so as to achieve equilibrium between supply and demand at the outset of the war, and stop the potential inflation before it had begun.

Keynes estimated the productive potential of the British economy as follows. Domestic output (calculated to be about £4,800 million in 1939) could be increased by soaking up the unemployed; by bringing into employment some non-active members of the population such as youths, women and the retired; and by more intensive work and overtime by those already employed. However, because of the drain of men into the armed forces, where they would not contribute to production, Keynes estimated that an increase in domestic output of only 15 per cent, or about £825 million in money terms, was possible. Net imports purchased by running down gold and foreign exchange reserves and by borrowing from abroad could be increased by approximately £350 million a year; while allowing buildings, plant and machinery to depreciate rather than replacing them might release a further £450 million a year for war consumption. Altogether, then, Keynes estimated that a maximum of £1,625 million worth of goods and services could be made available for the war effort without cutting into private consumption. This would not be adequate to finance the war-effort. Therefore, private consumption would have to be cut back. Keynes advocated a withdrawal of spending power by a combination of direct taxation on the wealthy, and a compulsory Capital Levy on those earning less than £5 per week.

Keynes' proposal of forced saving through a Capital Levy was, however, rejected by the Government on the grounds that the war-effort had to be based on consent rather than coercion. Instead, the government introduced selective rationing supported by price controls. The two instruments were complementary – rationing without price controls would have resulted in an increase in the price of rationed goods, and hurt the poor; while price controls without rationing would have resulted in shortages of the rationed goods. Rationing and price control of those goods considered necessities of life worked reasonably well in harness, and by 1941 they had been instituted comprehensively.

The gap between the cost of producing or importing the rationed commodities, and their retail price, increased as the war went on. The Government filled the gap by subsidies, the cost of which was met partly by increasing duties on alcohol and tobacco, and by raising Purchase Tax on goods not included in the cost-of-living index. This distorted the market allocation of goods in a way that would never have been considered in the First World War. However, the Government considered that rationing was a less socially disruptive way of achieving equality between aggregate supply and demand than inflation; and indeed, largely because the cost-of-living index was kept artificially low, the pressure for wage-increases and consequent industrial strife was much less than in World War One.

Despite the rejection of Keynes' specific solution for holding back private spending, the general principles advocated by Keynes for financing the war were adopted by the Government. Sir Kingsley Wood's 1941 Budget is generally regarded as the first Keynesian Budget, in that it was the first Budget which was consciously used as a means of managing the aggregate level of monetary demand. In the circumstances of 1941, the need was to hold back private consumption so that it would not be bidding against defence expenditure for the nation's resources.

The means used to achieve this end were increases in direct taxation. The standard rate of income tax was raised to 8s. 6d. in the £, and its exemption limits reduced. Later in the year, the rate of income tax was raised by a further 1s. 6d. to 10s. in the £, or 50 per cent. The Excess Profits Tax was raised from 60 per cent to 100 per cent in all industries, though it was later softened by various concessions including a 20 per cent post-war credit on tax paid. Indirect taxes were also raised; but the burden of financing the war fell increasingly on direct taxes, revenue from which had tripled by 1945 compared to its pre-war level.

In spite of the increases in taxation, revenue was not great enough to cover the increases in Government expenditure. In the period 1939–45, revenue covered only about half of total expenditure, and the gap had to be met by borrowing. Savings were switched from private uses to public (war) consumption partly by controls, which restricted the alternative investment opportunities, and partly by inducement. Private savings were transmitted to Government directly through its own institutions, such as the Post Office and Trustee Savings Bank, and indirectly through commercial banks. The commercial banks bought gilt-edged stock and short-term Treasury bills in increasing amounts, partly because so few alternative financial assets were available. By August 1945, Government stocks and cash constituted nearly 85 per cent of the assets of the British commercial banks.

The final means Government used to plug the financing gap was the rundown of foreign reserves. This proceeded much faster than Keynes had anticipated. Sterling balances of non-dollar countries held in London, valued at a total of £4,000 million, were frozen there for the duration of the war, providing the Government with much-needed foreign exchange. The problem of foreign exchange was conclusively solved by the Lend-Lease Agreement with the United States in 1941. From Lend-Lease, the British Government got imports of goods worth some £6,200 million. But Lend-Lease was a loan with strings attached, including a commitment on Britain's part to dismantle after the war the system of tariffs by which she gave preferential treatment to imports from the British Empire. Moreover, the fact that Britain had to let her own capital assets depreciate, and become dependent on American imports, shifted the balance of economic power between the two countries permanently in the U.S.A.'s favour.

After the war, the weakened British economy was run on the same principles as it had been during the war years. The post-war Labour Government maintained the structure of physical controls built up during the war. These controls directed the allocation of resources within the economy, and were complemented by Keynesian management of aggregate demand to keep the economy operating at close to full capacity. The need for revenue to finance Government's expenditure plans and complete the creation of the Welfare State determined taxation levels. The pre-war Treasury approach, by which the public's supposed tolerance of taxation set the upper limits to government expenditure, was thus decisively rejected. During the 1946–51 period, the current expenditure of public authorities averaged over £2,000 million a year, compared to just over £500 million p.a. in the decade before the Second World War. This represented a very substantial real increase, even though the purchasing power of money had fallen by somewhat over a third as compared to the pre-war years because of inflation.

Taxation revenue was insufficient to cover the full amount of public expenditure in the late 1940s. The Government Budget was in deficit of over £130 million a year in 1946–50. Far from responding to this deficit by making drastic cuts in its spending plans, as pre-war governments would have done, the post-war Labour Government met it by expanding the money supply. As a result of the plentiful supply of money, the rate of interest – the cost of borrowing money – was maintained at historically low levels. Interest rates were kept low as a deliberate policy, to stimulate investment financed from borrowed money, and to keep down the cost of servicing the National Debt. Thus, in 1946, the National Debt totalled £26,000 million, yet interest payments on it were only £500 million because of the low interest rates.

The Labour Government did extend public ownership, but only in industries which were, in the words of the Labour Party's 1945 manifesto, "ripe and over-ripe for public ownership". Nationalisation was not part of a coherent programme to transform the economy from a capitalist to a centrally-planned one. The industrial sectors which were nationalised were those in which government control had been extensive even before the Second World War.

The sectors which were nationalised divided into three main categories. The first was transport – road haulage, railways, and civil aviation – which had been extensively regulated in the inter-war years by Government in an effort to develop an integrated network.

The second main group nationalised were the public utilities of electricity and gas, which had previously been under municipal control. They were formally transferred from Local to Central Government so that the local systems could be tied together into a single national network. Other utilities which were already subject to extensive government regulation and which were formally nationalised by the Labour Government included radio, under the control of the British Broadcasting Corporation, and the central bank, the Bank of England, which was responsible for administering the issue of banknotes and gilt-edged stock on the Government's behalf.

The final group of industries which came under public ownership were the old staple industries of coal (nationalised in 1947) and iron and steel (taken over in 1949). These were industries which had made heavy losses during the inter-war depression and had relied heavily on government support during the 1930s. Each had suffered a substantial decline in its export market during the inter-war years. In each, inter-war governments had attempted to arrest the decline by keeping out imports through the imposition of tariffs, and by carving up the domestic market through the allocation of production quotas to each firm.

That the extension of public ownership was largely dictated by considerations of administrative efficiency rather than any desire to transform capitalism in Britain is indicated by the fact that the Conservatives, back in office after 1951, returned only road haulage and steel to private ownership. There was little opposition from private enterprise to the continued nationalisation of the remainder. Their former owners had received generous compensation; and under public ownership there was no move towards operating the firms along socialist lines, by, for example, the introduction of some form of workers' control. Thus, in 1956, of 272 Board members of the principal nationalised industries, 106 were directors of private businesses; 71 professional managers; and only 47 represented the Labour Party and trade unions.

The Conservative Government dismantled the remaining wartime controls on the economy. Otherwise, it attempted to regulate the economy very much as its predecessor had. Government spending actually increased under the Conservatives; but because of the growth of the private sector, Government spending as a proportion of national income fell slightly. The growth of National Income generated an increase in the government's taxation revenue, and the budget moved into surplus on the current account in the 1950s.

Like the 1945–51 Labour Government, the Conservative Government of 1951–64 tried to manage aggregate demand to maintain full employment in the economy. When the growth of national income was slowing down, Government expenditure was increased and taxation reduced. Conversely, a tighter budgetary policy was pursued when the growth of demand appeared to exceed the growth of productive capacity – the symptoms being inflation and a deficit on the Balance of Payments as more imports were drawn into the economy.

Keynes himself died in 1946, yet his ideas remained the cornerstone of British economic policy for the next quarter century.

With all its imperfections, the results of Keynesian economic policy were a dramatic improvement on those of the Treasury orthodoxy of the inter-war years. Even in the worst years of recession, unemployment during the years between 1948 and 1970 never rose above 2½ per cent of the work force, or one in forty; compared to more than one in ten unemployed throughout the inter-war years.

If the adoption of Keynesian techniques of demand management was not the sole, or even the principal, cause of the post-war prosperity, at the very least they can be credited with having underwritten and sustained that prosperity. If Keynesian techniques did not achieve perfect stability in the economy, at least they eliminated the violent fluctuations which had been experienced in the inter-war years. The knowledge that the government would act to prevent a rise in unemployment above 2½ per cent of the labour force reinforced confidence in the economic system, and encouraged the investment essential to the attainment of economic growth.

The adoption of Keynesian techniques of economic management, like the advances in the provision of social services, was forced upon the government by the imperatives of war. The experience of the war years proved that some measure of government planning and intervention could assist in the more efficient operation of a capitalist economy, and it put lie to the negative thinking which had pervaded economic policy-making during the 1930s.

IV

When the dust settled over the Second World War, the balance of world power had fundamentally altered.

Britain was accepted as one of the "Big Three" allies, with the United States and the Soviet Union, and determined the shape of the peace with them at the Yalta and Potsdam conferences. But in truth, Britain's economy was already too weak to support such a world role, and it could not be propped up indefinitely by her geographically disparate Empire.

Cracks were already appearing in the British Empire before the Second World War. Its dissolution commenced shortly afterwards, when India, the most populous of the British dominions, was granted independence in 1947. During the 1950s, the Conservative Government continued the policy of decolonisation. Although decolonisation was opposed by a minority on the right of the Conservative Party, it enjoyed majority support from both major political parties.

The bipartisan approach to foreign policy was seriously threatened only once, at the time of the Suez crisis in 1956. The Prime Minister at the time was Anthony Eden, who decided to go to war against Egypt after she had nationalised the Suez Canal, the main link for shipping between the Mediterranean and the Indian Ocean. The abortive campaign proved to be the last spasm of the British Empire. Eden's policy was strongly attacked by the Labour Party, and was not even fully supported by his own Cabinet. It isolated Britain from other members of the western alliance, who did not feel that nationalisation of the canal was sufficient justification for war. The fiasco of Suez cost Eden his office. It also provided dramatic evidence that Britain could no longer stand alone in the world as she had before the Second World War. Britain's security depended on alliance with other nations – and the nations with whom she chose to ally herself were the industrial nations of the capitalist West.

Britain's role in the western alliance diminished as the post-war years rolled on. In the late 1950s, Harold Macmillan grandiosely conceived Britain as being at the centre of the "three interlocking circles" of the western alliance. The first circle was the Atlantic alliance with the other great English-speaking power, the United States, institutionalised in the North Atlantic Treaty Organisation (NATO). The second circle was the emergent British Commonwealth, formed from the newly independent nations of the old British Empire. The third circle was Western Europe – Britain remained outside the European Economic Community of France, Italy, West Germany and the Benelux countries; but she was the pivot of a second customs union, the European Free Trade Association, formed by seven nations on the periphery of the Community.

The "three circles" concept appeared increasingly anachronistic during the 1960s as Britain's relative economic strength declined. Yet the political leaders accepted the diminution of Britain's world role only with great reluctance. Defence remained the single largest item of public expenditure, and soaked up more than one-twentieth of her Gross National Product at a time when more dynamic economies such as West Germany and Japan were directing their resources to productive investment instead of armaments. Britain's consequential decline eventually forced her leaders to accept that Britain's future lay as a rather junior partner in the European Economic Community, and not as a world power in her own right.

Entry into the European Economic Community was opposed by both the left wing of the Labour Party and the right wing of the Conservative Party, because of the constraints it would place on Britain's sovereignty. The Labour left foresaw that membership of the E.E.C. would tie Britain more tightly to the capitalist economic system; while the Conservative right refused to accept that Britain could no longer stand alone in the world. But the opponents of E.E.C. membership were outmanoeuvred by the liberal wings of the Labour and Conservative Parties. In 1975, a Referendum was held which confirmed Britain's membership of the Community by a majority of two to one. The Referendum was the last great achievement of the consensus politicians; the last time they cut across Party lines to achieve an overwhelming majority in favour of a single policy.

A bipartisan foreign policy was the third leg of the tripod on which the age of consensus was founded, along with the Welfare State and a Keynesian economic policy.

The fundamental premise on which the age of consensus was founded was that managed capitalism, as it existed in post-war Britain, was a beneficent and benevolent system. Ten years after the Second World War had ended, Anthony Crosland wrote *The Future of Socialism*. Crosland's central thesis was that, because of the transformation which had taken place in the preceding twenty years, British capitalism in the post-war era was a fundamentally different animal from the system which had existed before 1939. Crosland wrote:

> Socialists in the 1930s, whatever their disagreements on long-term questions, were united on the immediate objectives of a majority Labour Government. These were first the abolition of poverty and the creation of a social service state; secondly, a greater equalisation of wealth; and thirdly, greater economic planning for full employment and stability. But many socialists, while assenting to these aims in principle, did so in a distinctly pessimistic frame of mind, thinking them probably unattainable within the existing economic framework. They believed, on the basis of a predominantly Marxist analysis, that capitalism itself must first be forcibly overthrown.

Crosland went on to argue that the experience of the post-war years had belied the pessimism of the inter-war socialists, and proved that the objectives of socialism could be attained without State ownership of all the nation's capital. Absolute poverty had been abolished. A social service state and greater economic planning had been introduced. The major task of socialism still remaining was the greater equalisation of wealth – but in Crosland's view, the abolition of private property was not necessary to achieve this. The means Crosland proposed to achieve greater social equality were essentially twofold – firstly, greater social spending to help the worst-off sections of society; and secondly, a series of fiscal measures designed to equalise the status and privileges of different groups in society.

Crosland believed that high levels of social spending could be financed out of the proceeds of economic growth, without significantly raising the incidence of taxation. He also believed that continuing economic growth would mean that the five Giants Beveridge saw on the road to reconstruction would soon be overcome, and the whole population of Britain would be adequately housed, educated and cared for.

> If our present rate of economic growth continues, material want and poverty and deprivation of essential goods will gradually cease to be a problem. We shall increasingly need to focus attention, not on universal categories, but on individual persons and families – not on the economic causes of distress, but on the social and psychological ones.

Higher social spending would not of itself be sufficient to eradicate class-consciousness in Britain, however. In Crosland's view,

> Greater social equality in Britain will require a more egalitarian educational system, and a greater equality in the pattern of consumption. But it will also [to break up class barriers] call for a further redistribution of inherited wealth, an equalisation of power and privilege within industry.
>
> *The Future of Socialism*, p.257.

Crosland then went on to propose a battery of policies to achieve these objectives. In the educational sphere, he recommended that the public schools should be gradually integrated into the State system. The redistribution of inherited wealth could be brought about by death duties, supplemented by high marginal rates of tax on unearned income, and by the taxation of company dividend payments rather than profits, to encourage the reinvestment of corporate earnings.

The outstanding feature of the vision of a "socialist" society offered by Crosland was that it contained very little that a progressive Tory would object to in principle. No doubt a Conservative would lay rather less weight on the desirability of equalising wealth; but this was a difference of emphasis rather than of substance. The basis of Crosland's vision was exactly the same as that offered by the Conservative Party – a property-owning democracy, in which the ownership of industrial capital remained predominantly in private hands.

Crosland, in common with the rest of the Revisionist wing of the Labour Party, felt that nationalisation of industry had gone far enough by 1950. Further nationalisation should take place, if at all, only if the economic case for it was clearly made out. He also argued that nationalisation should be by individual firms, not by entire industrial sectors, and defined the economic case for nationalising particular firms in rather narrow terms.

> An economic improvement may follow from public ownership where an existing industry is clearly performing poorly; where competition either cannot or is not permitted to enforce an improvement; where physical or fiscal controls are incapable of curing the situation; and where public ownership will not bring attendant disadvantages of its own.
>
> *The Future of Socialism* p. 477.

There was no support here for the vision offered by the Bevanite Left of the public sector as the leading sector of the economy, dominating its "commanding heights". Nor was there any support for a radical change in the structure of power within either public or private corporations. Crosland rejected the idea that the Board of Directors of private companies should include either nominees of the Government or elected representatives of the work forces. He did not even consider the proposals of the Left for institutional changes within the public corporations, so that instead of being run by private businessmen drafted in for the purpose of operating essentially capitalist enterprises along hierarchical lines, they would be run as workers' co-operatives by a Board containing representatives elected by the workers and ultimately accountable to them. Nor did Crosland support the notion that the "efficiency" of nationalised corporations should be evaluated in broader terms than narrow financial performance – for example, the economy and the social-value-added by the corporation, in which the wages earned by the work force would be interpreted as a plus (adding to national income) and not as a minus (subtracting from private profit).

Crosland advocated State intervention in industry only where it would improve commercial efficiency, and not as a means of altering the structure of economic power. This approach was wholly consistent with that of the liberal Butler–Macmillan wing of the

Conservative Party. Particular private firms, such as Rolls Royce and British Leyland, were brought into public ownership, but only when they were on the verge of bankruptcy and the alternative was their liquidation.

In general, the consensus approach was to seek to regulate private industry so that it would serve broader social interests, rather than intervene in it directly. However, the overall impact of State regulations on monopolistic practices in private industry was negligible. Moreover, this was inevitable, given the social democratic philosophy behind the regulations. Social democratic governments could not consistently act so as to protect the individual consumer against exploitation by capitalist enterprise, because the fundamental premise of social democracy was that capitalist enterprise was the best obtainable system for organising the production, distribution and exchange of goods, so that if it was threatened, it would only give way to something worse.

For this reason, the governments of the era of consensus in Britain did not act to reduce the concentration of wealth. At the end of the 1960s, the top one-hundredth of the population owned a third of the total wealth of the country; and the top one-twentieth owned well over a half. The concentration of wealth had diminished somewhat since 1945, and analysis of the statistics showed that the major reasons for the diminution were the growth of home ownership and of institutional savings for life insurance and for pensions. However, investment by the savings institutions was controlled by a very few people at the top of them. Thus, the concentration of power over industrial capital was left intact.

The Crosland version of social democracy envisaged the gradual improvement of the living-standards and relative status of the working class by directing the proceeds of economic growth towards them. In this way, it was hoped, the concentration of economic wealth and power in a few hands could gradually be eroded without anyone being worse off in absolute terms. This approach could work only so long as economic growth was sustained. If there was no growth, then the redistribution of wealth towards the relatively poor – the 90 per cent of the population who between them owned less than a third of the nation's wealth – could occur only if some of the wealth of the top 10 per cent was actually taken from them. If this happened, the interests of the owners of capital would no longer be consistent with those of the rest of society; and one group could only improve its position at the expense of the others. This conflict would strike at the very foundations of the era of consensus.

In its failure to appreciate the potential conflict inherent within post-war capitalism, Crosland's analysis was flawed because it was static. His conclusion that post-war British capitalism was a benevolent system was true only for the particular point in time when he was writing. It is true that the position of the poorest 90 per cent of the population had improved by 1956 as compared to the inter-war years. But what Crosland failed to recognise was that this transformation had come about, not because of any logic inherent within the capitalist system, but because of the accident of war. Only under the impact of the Second World War had the ruling élite in Britain made concessions to the have-nots, in order to mobilise their support for the execution of the war. There was nothing inevitable about this process – the concessions were only made because they were the lesser of two evils. The alternative was defeat, and the conquest of Britain by a foreign power, which would have destroyed the British Establishment entirely.

Chapter Two

THE STRUGGLE IN THE LABOUR MARKET 1965–1979

And we are here as on a darkling plain
Swept with confused alarms of struggle and flight,
Where ignorant armies clash by night.

Matthew Arnold, 'Dover Beach'

I

After the Second World War, both the Conservative Party and the Labour Party attempted to win support beyond their traditional class bases. Both accepted the framework of the Welfare State to provide minimum living standards for all, and Keynesian economic policy to sustain high aggregate demand and employment. Within this framework, Conservative Governments placed more emphasis on policies designed to foster initiative and incentives for business, while Labour Governments tended to be more concerned with social justice and equality of opportunity. That is to say, each party tended to promote policies which would improve the relative position of its own supporters. But these differences were marginal, because sustained growth of output and earnings meant that every social group could improve its real income year by year, without detriment to other social groups. The size of the national cake was getting larger, so everyone could get a bigger slice. Indeed, it was in the interests of a government party seeking to remain in office to ensure that as many people as possible got a bigger slice. In consequence, both parties when in government – the Conservative Party in 1951–64, and the Labour Party in 1964–70 – attempted to act, not exclusively in the interests of their own supporters, but in the "national interest". The outstanding performance of the British economy by historical standards during the 1951–70 period meant that they could do this without harming the interests of their own supporters.

There was one cloud on the horizon, however. While the British economy grew more rapidly in the 1951–70 period than it ever had before, its rate of growth was low by comparison with other Western European economies. During the 1950s, the relatively slow growth of the British economy by international standards did not cause much concern. The continental economies and Japan were, after all, recovering from wartime devastation much worse than that experienced by victorious Britain. Furthermore, at the beginning of the Second World War, Britain had already been a mature industrial economy, with less than one-tenth of the working population employed in agriculture. By contrast, countries such as Japan, France and Italy still had large rural populations, on which the industrial sector could draw at relatively low wages. The industrial sectors in these countries therefore faced no shortage of labour in their effort to catch up with the more advanced industry of Britain and the United States.

But by the end of the 1960s the reassuring "catch up" hypothesis was exploded. The economies of France, West Germany and Japan had all caught up and overtaken the British economy, and were still growing faster than it. It was becoming increasingly clear that the poor performance of the British economy in international terms was not a temporary phenomenon, which would last only for as long as it took the Western European and Japanese economies to catch up with it. Rather, Britain was in secular decline. This decline was reflected in her diminishing role in world politics from the heady days at the end of the Second World War when Britain had taken her place at the conference table with the superpowers, the United States and the Soviet Union.

What really brought home the weakness of Britain in the 1960s, however, was not her diminished position in international conferences but the chronic weakness of her Balance of Payments. In the early 1950s Britain had accounted for one-fifth of the world's exports of manufactured goods. By the end of the 1960s her share of the world's manufactured exports had fallen to a tenth. At the same time, Britain herself was importing more manufactured goods.

The single most important reason for Britain's poor performance in world trade was a decline in her price competitiveness. Inflation in Britain averaged about 3 per cent p.a. during the 1953–66 period, which was roughly 1 per cent more than her main trading partners; so the cost of British exports was increasing, while the cost of foreign imports in Britain fell relatively to the cost of home-produced goods.

During this period, the rate of inflation of the major industrial economies was related to the increase in their wage-costs per unit of output. The countries with the largest increases in wages per unit of output also had the largest increases in final prices. The rise in money wages in Britain was not out of line with the increases in West Germany or Japan. However, the increase in productivity in British industry was much lower than in these economies; and this slow growth in productivity was the main reason for Britain's high rate of inflation compared to her competitors.

The problem for the Wilson Government which took office in 1964 was that there was no simple way of improving the productivity of British industry. The new Government could have opted for devaluation of the £ sterling, which would have reduced the cost of British exports in foreign currencies, while correspondingly increasing the cost of sterling of foreign imports into Britain. However, devaluation would have given only a once-off advantage to British industry on world markets, and this advantage would have been gradually eroded if the ratio of wage-costs per unit of output had continued to increase in Britain more rapidly than in her main trading partners.

The Wilson Government opted instead for an incomes policy, with the intention of keeping wage increases to the same level as the growth in productivity, so that wage costs per unit of output would remain constant and the general rise in prices would be restrained. The Wilson Government set up a National Board of Prices and Incomes in 1965 with the responsibility for monitoring the implementation of the "norm" of between 3 per cent and 3½ per cent the Government set for pay increases for the twelve months from May 1965 to May 1966.

This first attempt at pay restraint was not successful; in the year May 1965–May 1966 average earnings rose not 3½ per cent but 8 per cent. By July 1966 the Government was faced with serious Balance of Payments difficulties and a run on the pound. It responded to these difficulties by introducing a general package to deflate the economy and reduce the volume of imports, including a statutory wage freeze for six months.

The freeze was followed in January 1967 by a more flexible policy. The new norm for pay increases was set at zero, but four possible exceptions were allowed – two on economic grounds, two on grounds of equity. The economic grounds admissible were where workers made a "direct contribution towards increasing productivity" or where an increase in pay was required to attract manpower to a particular expanding sector of the economy. The equitable exceptions were an increase in pay made for the lowest-paid workers in a firm; and an increase in pay introduced in order to correct a gross anomaly. These guidelines remained in force until the first half of 1968. Actual earnings increased during this period by about 6 per cent. In 1968–69, the Government set a ceiling of 3½ per cent p.a., and actual earnings increased by a further 8 per cent during this period.

This was hardly a record of success. One reason was that the norms were established on the assumption that retail prices would remain stable. In fact, during the four years 1965–68 retail prices rose by 4 per cent per annum on average; which meant that money wages had to increase by at least this amount to maintain their real purchasing power.

The mechanism by which earnings rose faster than the stipulated norms was that of "wage drift". During the 1950s actual earnings had risen more or less in line with wage rates, which were negotiated on an industry-wide level between trade unions and the major employers. During the 1960s negotiated wage rates stayed broadly within the guidelines laid down by the Labour Government, but actual wages drifted above the negotiated wage rates. In the course of the 1960s, actual wages rose nearly three times as fast as wage rates.

The difference between wage earnings and wage rates was made up of three main elements in total earnings – firstly, piecework, or bonus payments made under payments-by-results systems, which nearly half of all workers in the manufacturing sector earned; secondly, overtime earnings; and thirdly, plant rates paid in particular factories of large firms over and above the agreed company-wide rate. These three elements in wage drift were very difficult to control within the context of a national incomes policy, even in the rare cases where they were referred to the Prices and Incomes Board.

The reason for this difficulty was spelt out in the Report of the Donovan Commission on Industrial Relations, which was set up by the Labour Government in 1965 and delivered its Report to Government in 1968. The Commission identified a two-tier bargaining structure in the British labour market. The upper tier was the formal structure, recognised by law, where bargaining took place between paid union officials and employers at industry level. The second tier was informal, and not subject to regulation by the law. It was highly decentralised, taking place at shop-floor level between shop stewards representing the work-force on the one hand, and plant managers representing the employers on the other, with both acting largely independently of their national organisations.

The policies of the Labour Government assisted the growth of the informal tier. Wage rates at national level were held back by incomes policy, while aggregate demand continued to be buoyant and retail prices continued to rise. The circumstances were similar to those existing in the labour market during the two World Wars, when the official trade union structure became in effect an instrument through which the Government sought to regulate the economy, rather than an independent organisation acting in the interests of its own members. The consequence was that ordinary trade unionists were left with the option of either accepting the wage rates their unions negotiated on their behalf and seeing the real value of their earnings eroded by inflation; or seeking to maintain the real value of their earnings through unofficial action. They chose the latter option, with the result that the unofficial shop stewards movement gained in importance in the British labour market. It was the only effective instrument through which workers could protect their living standards in a period of collaboration between the official trade unions and the Government.

Shop stewards used the one real exception in the Labour Government's incomes policy to advance their members' position. This exception was productivity bargaining. For the Government, productivity bargaining had obvious attractions. As has been pointed out, the reason for Britain's relatively high rate of inflation in the early and mid-1960s was not an excessive rate of increase in wages per se, but rather an excessive rate of increase in wages *relative to* increase in output. A productivity bargain in theory restored the link between wages and output, by making the size of the wage-packet depend on the volume of output a worker produced.

In practice, productivity bargaining rarely worked like this. One of the members of the Donovan Commission, Lord McCarthy, has commented that "piece-work wage structures provide shop stewards with unrivalled opportunities for influence". The reason was that piece-rates, by their very nature, had to be set up at shop-floor level, according to the type of machine being operated by the workers. If a company appointed a work-study engineer to fix a standard rate for a particular job, it was the shop steward rather than an outside trade union official with whom he negotiated. It was also the shop steward who negotiated the size of bonus payment for production over and above the standard rate. By virtue of his position as the representative of the work-force on the shop-floor, the shop steward was in a vastly superior position to that of an outside trade union official in knowing what would be a fair rate for a given job on a particular machine. Perhaps even more importantly from the point of view of management, the shop stewards were also in a better position than union officials to know what rate would be acceptable to the shop-floor workers.

It was because payments-by-results systems were established on the basis of acceptability rather than technical efficiency that they were liable to degenerate and become means by which unearned pay increases were obtained, rather than by which genuine incentives were given to efficiency.

It should be emphasised that in the vast majority of cases neither management nor the official trade union movement strongly objected to the growth of shop steward influence as such; indeed, in most cases they positively welcomed it. From the trade unions' point of view, shop stewards were a useful unpaid element in the organisation, performing routine chores such as recruiting new workers to the union, collecting their subscriptions to the union, dealing with minor complaints and more generally acting as a link between the shop-floor worker in the factory and the official trade union hierarchy outside. From the point of view of plant management, shop stewards were likely to have a better understanding of the problems facing the plant, and reflect the attitudes of the workers in it more acurately, than outside officials. Consequently, shop stewards were generally a better means for the regulation of the work-force than trade union officials. One of the less publicised results of the Donovan Report was that nearly three-quarters (72 per cent) of the managers interviewed in the course of the Commission's investigations stated that their shop stewards were reluctant to push strike action; only 4 per cent of the managers interviewed stated that their shop stewards were "very ready" to advocate a strike.

The real problem with the informal system of collective bargaining as far as the Donovan Commission was concerned was that, largely by accident, it came into conflict with the formal system, and thereby made worse the very problems with which the collective bargaining process was supposed to deal. The piecemeal and uncoordinated nature of shop-floor bargaining increased the likelihood of anomalies appearing in the pay structures of different shop-floors within the same industry, and even within the same firm. It also gave rise to quite arbitrary differences in collective bargaining procedures. These anomalies, Donovan argued, themselves generated industrial discontent and were in part responsible for the growth in the number of unofficial strikes, not sanctioned by the relevant trade union.

The obvious conclusion from this would seem to be that the Labour Government should leave well alone, and not attempt to regulate the labour market. The regulation of the formal trade union tier through incomes policy had merely given rise to the growth of an informal shop steward tier, as it had during the years of the two World Wars. By attempting to regulate the outcome of the process of bargaining in the labour market – that is, the level of pay settlements – the Government had unintentionally altered the process itself, because it had not acted on the underlying forces within the market. Like a balloon which has been squeezed at one point, these forces reappeared, in altered form, at another point.

In fairness to Donovan, his Commission was prevented from arriving at a conclusion which was directly critical of incomes policy by its original terms of reference. The Commission had been instructed by Government to "consider relations between managements and employees and the role of trade unions and employers' associations in promoting the interests of their members and in accelerating the social and economic advance of the nation, with particular reference to the law affecting the activities of these bodies, and to report". In other words, the Commission's job was to analyse the process of collective bargaining in Britain, and not the forces underlying that process. Its Report presented in 1968 represented a reasonable attempt to do that job. It identified the anomalies arising from the structure of collective bargaining in Britain, and concluded that the development of the informal shop-floor tier alongside the formal industry-wide tier of collective bargaining was the proximate cause of those anomalies. What it failed to do was answer the question of *why* this development had taken place. But within the limitations of its own analysis, it came to a sensible conclusion. If the problem was the development of a two-tier structure and the growth of informal agreements between shop stewards and relatively junior representatives of management, then the solution was the creation of a single tier of collective bargaining at plant or company level, and the introduction of greater formality in collectively bargained agreements and corresponding reduction in the area governed by "custom and practice".

The Donovan Commission put the main emphasis on voluntary reform in collective bargaining procedures to bring about the changes they thought were necessary. Legislation could play a useful supplementary role, and the Commission proposed the introduction of an Industrial Relations Act to assist the process of reform at plant level, by requiring companies above a certain size to register their collective agreements with the Department of Employment and Productivity. The idea of registration was that it would encourage the development of greater formality in collective bargaining. The Commission also proposed the creation of an Industrial Relations Board "to investigate and report upon cases and problems arising out of registration" and upon other matters of industrial relations, where they were so requested.

The role of the law as envisaged by Donovan was passive. Any more active approach was fraught with danger, for, the Donovan Report concluded, "at the present time legislation making procedure agreements enforceable would not in fact be enforced, and like all legislation that is not enforced would bring the law into disrepute". However, as far as the Wilson Government was concerned in 1968, the passive approach advocated by Donovan was not acceptable. The Government's incomes policy was in tatters. The deflationary measures taken in July 1966 had succeeded in avoiding the devaluation of sterling for only sixteen months. In November 1967 sterling was devalued from $2.80 to $2.40. In order for devaluation to work, the volume of imports had to be held back, requiring the continuance of deflationary policies; while the volume of exports had to grow. Exports would only grow if they retained the advantage devaluation had given them and remained competitive in their price with foreign-produced goods. This in turn required that wage costs did not run ahead of output – the very problem that the Government had first tried to tackle three years earlier.

By 1968, then, it was politically imperative for the Wilson Government to act. Their former economic policies, directed towards maintaining the parity of sterling by restraining the growth in money wages and improving the level of industrial productivity, had failed and had been seen to fail. Public opinion polls indicated that the Government's popularity had slumped to an all-time low and that it faced overwhelming defeat in the event of a General Election.

So the Government introduced a White Paper, "In Place of Strife", in January 1969, which set out its proposals for the reform of industrial relations in Britain. "In Place of Strife" incorporated the Donovan Commission's recommendation that a Commission for Industrial Relations should be set up to act as an umpire in industrial relations disputes, between trade unions. However, to give teeth to the proposed Commission, "In Place of Strife" suggested that fines should be imposed on employers who refused to recognise a union it recommended, and also on trade unions which obstructed employers who recognised another union for collective bargaining purposes. This was the first controversial proposal. In addition, the Secretary of State for Employment and Productivity would have the power to impose a "conciliation pause" of 28 days on workers involved in a dispute, during which both they and their employers would be compelled to revert to the status quo and return to work. The idea of the conciliation pause was to reduce the incidence of so-called wildcat strikes which flared up for often trivial reasons. A compulsory conciliation period would, it was hoped, allow tempers to cool and enable the settlement of many disputes without any stoppage.

The final controversial provision of "In Place of Strife" was that the Secretary of State for Employment and Productivity would have the discretionary power in the event of major official strikes to order a secret ballot of trade union members to ensure that a majority were in favour of the strike. In all cases, the legislation would be supported by the threat of fines against any party which refused to obey it.

The idea behind "In Place of Strife" was to encourage the rationalisation of collective bargaining procedures in Britain. But from the outset, there were doubts among some of the leading figures of the Labour movement as to whether legislation supported by the threat of fines – and, presumably, imprisonment for an offending party who refused to pay the fine – was the right way to go about this rationalisation. These doubts had been shared by the members of the Donovan Commission. In the Cabinet, the doubters were led by the Home Secretary, James Callaghan. In an attempt to out-manoeuvre this potential opposition, the Prime Minister, Harold Wilson, deliberately by-passed the ad hoc Cabinet Committee on industrial relations, and attempted to push the proposals of "In Place of Strife" through main Cabinet directly.

However, this tactical ploy failed to dampen the opposition. Outside Parliament, feeling was hardening among the largest trade unions against the Bill's penal clauses. The historical ties between the trade unions and the Parliamentary Labour Party, many of whose members were sponsored by trade unions, meant that the trade unions were in a very effective position to put their point of view. They formed the single most important base of support for Labour Members of Parliament; so that if the Labour Government's policies upset the trade unions, they would undermine the position of the M.P.s themselves.

Instead of an extension of Government interference in the labour market, the trade unions proposed a strengthening of the power of the Trade Unions Congress to intervene in disputes that threatened the jobs of union members not engaged in the dispute. In particular, it was proposed that for the first time the T.U.C. would have the right to intervene in unofficial disputes, which had previously, by definition, been outside the scope of official trade union regulation.

Few ministers of the Labour Government believed that the T.U.C.'s intervention would be effective in curbing the growth of unofficial strikes. But in the end the hard facts of power politics won the day. A sufficient number of back-bench Labour M.P.s were convinced by the T.U.C.'s case, and alarmed by the prospect of a split between the Parliamentary Party and the trade union movement outside Parliament, to make the passage of the Industrial Relations Bill highly unlikely. On June 18th, 1969, the Government's Chief Whip informed the Prime Minister that he could not ensure enough support in the Select Committee of the House of Commons considering the Bill to get the Bill through Committee stage and on to the floor of the House.

It was the end. The Prime Minister, Harold Wilson, and his Secretary of State for Employment and Productivity, Barbara Castle, were faced with the option of resigning or of conceding defeat over their Industrial Relations Bill. They chose to concede defeat and live to fight another day. A face-saving "solemn and binding agreement" was drawn up between the T.U.C. General Council on the one hand, and Wilson and Castle for the Government on the other, by which the T.U.C. pledged itself to control unofficial disputes among its members more effectively.

Predictably enough, the agreement was totally unsuccessful. The number of working days lost through strikes in Britain, which had averaged just over 3 million days per year during the period 1960–67, and had risen to 4½ million in 1968, increased further to nearly 7 million in 1969, and 11 million in 1970. The Government's attempts at restraining wages were abandoned, and the increase in money wages increased to more than 10 per cent year-on-year for the first time since the Second World War – although most of the increase was eaten up by increases in prices, so that the increase in the real value of earnings was no greater than it had been in previous years during the 1960s.

On June 18th, 1970, exactly one year after the Government's Chief Whip had informed his leader of the majority against the Industrial Relations Bill in Committee, the Labour Government was defeated at the polls by the Conservative Party in the General Election. The hard fact was that the Labour Government's economic policies had failed. Its one success was to get the Balance of Payments back into the black after the 1967 devaluation of sterling. But the advantages conferred on British exporters by devaluation were being rapidly eroded by the acceleration in prices and wages, and the increase in the number of working days lost through strikes.

The conventional view was that the Labour Government had been right to intervene in the labour market in Britain to attempt to solve these problems. Many proponents of this view felt that the Labour Government had failed, not because its policies were wrong, but because of its historical relationship with the trade union movement, and the pressure the trade unions were consequently able to exert to undermine the policies of the Government. Thus Peter Jenkins, in his analysis of the fight over "In Place of Strife", concluded that, "The Social Democratic dilemma – how to contain the interests of organised labour within a broadly-based political party, and how to combine free trade unionism within the efficient management of a mixed economy – remained unsolved." (Peter Jenkins, *The Battle of Downing Street*.)

But there is an alternative analysis. It is that Government

intervention in the labour market was almost totally irrelevant as a means of solving the problems with which it purported to deal. Wage pressure, so far from being the cause of inflation in retail prices, was rather a response to it and an attempt on the part of workers to defend their living standards. As for unofficial strikes, Government policies were probably themselves the single most important cause of their increase.

Further, even had incomes policy been successful in holding back money wages, it would have made no contribution towards correcting the fundamental cause of the poor performance of the British economy compared to its major international competitors. Britain's fundamental problem in the post-war era has been the slow rate of growth of her productive capacity, not the rate of growth of her money wages.

The 1964–70 Labour Government's intervention in the labour market was actually counter-productive. The Government's goal in its incomes policy was to keep increases in money wages in line with what could be paid from improvements in productivity. In its proposed industrial relations reform, the Government's goal was to rationalise the operation of the labour market in Britain, and in particular to eliminate the incidence of unofficial strikes.

These were laudable objectives but, unfortunately, they were not interpreted as such by the workers whose consent to them was essential if they were to be successful. Much of the work-force perceived the policies as a threat to their living standards – a direct threat in the case of incomes policy, which attempted to hold back their money wages; and an indirect threat in the case of industrial relations reform, which would undermine the power of workers to bargain with management through their trade unions over their wages and working conditions. The industrial work-force reacted to this threat by trying to defend itself, by evading the incomes policies; and by directly opposing legal reform of the machinery of industrial relations in Britain. And because of this reaction, the Labour Government's policies resulted in an increase in industrial unrest.

The lesson that should have been drawn from this experience was that future Governments should not attempt to extend regulation of the labour market. The potential benefits from such regulation in no way justified the potential costs in terms of industrial unrest. But as the new Conservative Government took office in June of 1970, this lesson had not yet been learnt.

II

The Conservative Government of Edward Heath entered office in June 1970, committed to reducing the rate of inflation. The new Government believed, correctly, that the single most important reason for the defeat of the Labour Government at the 1970 election was its failure to deal with the problem of inflation in Britain. It also believed, incorrectly, that this failure was a consequence of the Labour Party's historic links with the trade union movement, which prevented it from intervening effectively in the "general interest" in the labour market. On this single, fundamental error of analysis rests the history of the Heath Government.

The Conservative Party has always been less sympathetic to the imposition of physical controls or direct government intervention in the economy than has the Labour Party. The Conservative Party is, after all, the Party of those who have done well out of the market system, so it is predisposed to view the workings of free markets as generally beneficent. The Government's role, in Conservative ideology, is to hold the ring and to ensure that bargaining between sellers and buyers in free markets takes place on a fair basis.

This approach manifested itself in the Heath Government's labour market policy. It did not favour incomes policy, as had its predecessor. The Prices and Incomes Board was wound up, and attempts to influence directly the level of pay settlements in the private sector were discontinued. The level of pay in the private sector was, as far as the new Government was concerned, a matter to be agreed between the employers and employees, the buyers and the sellers of labour.

In the public sector, the Government was directly involved in pay bargaining as the employer. In October 1970 the Heath Government laid down guidelines for the level of public sector pay settlements in the form of the "N-1" policy. The notion behind this policy was that each pay award in the public sector should be 1 per cent lower than the previous one, so that pay rises would be gradually brought down to the level sustainable by the underlying growth of the economy, and at the same time set an example of wage restraint to the private sector.

The form of the "N-1" policy reveals how out of touch the new Government was with the way in which the labour market in Britain functions. Typically, pay bargaining takes place during the course of an annual pay round which runs from August to July. One of the main criteria used by union negotiators in establishing the target for the pay award they demand for their members is comparability; that is, union negotiators are concerned that the position of their members relative to that of other groups of workers in comparable jobs does not suffer. Thus, if the going rate of wage increases for manual labourers in a given pay round is 5 per cent, a union negotiator will be very reluctant to accept a substantially lower settlement for his members. If he does, he will be seen to have failed, and his authority among the rank-and-file membership will be undermined. Yet the "N-1" policy required the trade union negotiators to do just this – to accept lower settlements later in the pay round than comparable groups of workers who had settled earlier. In consequence, the application of the "N-1" policy to the public sector provoked resistance from the unions, and resulted in a number of damaging strikes. In December 1970, a strike in the electrical supply industry led the Government to declare a State of Emergency and enforce a rota system of power cuts all over the country. This was followed by a long and bitter postal strike. The fact that the Government "won" the strike, in the sense that the final settlement was closer to the Government's original offer than to the union's demand, is of less importance than the fact that it could have been avoided altogether with a better-structured incomes policy, or indeed with no incomes policy at all.

However, the "N-1" policy was only the secondary component of the Heath Government's attempt to influence the workings of the labour market. The most important component was their Industrial Relations Bill, which was presented to Parliament in December 1970, and after a stormy passage became law the following August.

Conservative philosophy extols the virtues of free enterprise, and the untrammelled workings of the free market. It is true that after the Second World War, under the influence of its liberal wing, the Conservative Party accepted the extension of the role of Government in the economy – in the provision of social services and in the regulation of the overall level of demand to sustain full employment. However, beyond these limits, the Conservative view remained that the interaction of buyers' demand and sellers' supply in the free market brings about the best possible allocation of commodities.

The problem in the labour market, in the Heath Government's view, was that the free play of the forces of supply and demand was distorted by the monopoly over the supply of labour held by trade unions. By virtue of that monopoly, the trade unions were, in the Conservatives' view, in a position to push up wages beyond the level justified by the productivity of labour. The upward pressure the trade unions were able to exert on wages was, in this analysis, the major cause of price inflation in Britain and the progressive erosion of her competitive position.

The Industrial Relations Act of 1971 was an attempt to reform the labour market and eliminate its major distortions. The Act gave workers the statutory right to belong or not to belong to trade unions, as they chose. By placing the two on an equal footing, the Act struck directly against the closed shop, which was the requirement in most unionised companies in Britain that workers join the trade union representing the work-force in that company. The closed shop was the foundation of trade union power; without it, the unions' ability to negotiate wage increases, supported by the right to strike, would be seriously undermined. If a high proportion of the work-force of a firm was non-unionised, then the union's capacity to organise an effective strike would be reduced. The closed shop was something for which the trade unions had fought long and hard, and the end of the closed shop implied a major shift of power in the collective bargaining process away from the trade unions and towards the employers. For this reason, it was bound to provoke a backlash from the trade union movement. The question was whether the Government could ride out this backlash.

A further controversial provision in the 1971 Industrial Relations Act was the limitations it placed on legal immunities from damages arising from strikes. The Act provided that only registered trade unions and their agents (i.e. trade union officials) could induce persons to break contracts in furtherance of a trade dispute. This provision at once attacked shop steward power, by making shop stewards liable for damages caused by unofficial strikes, and was an inducement to trade unions to register under the Act so that they would escape liability for strikes.

The clauses for the enforcement of the Industrial Relations Act were similar in substance with those proposed in "In Place of Strife". Trade unions and employers' associations were required to register with a Registrar of Trade Unions and Employers' Organisations. Unregistered unions would be liable for unlimited damages, and would lose certain valuable tax rebates. Collective bargaining agreements were enforceable in law, unless a written provision by the parties to the agreement stated otherwise, and a new National Industrial Relations Court was established to deal with matters relating to collective bargaining issues and to act as a court of appeal from the existing Industrial Tribunals. The general intention behind all these measures was the introduction of greater formality into collective bargaining, and the reduction of the incidence of unofficial disputes.

Finally, the Act contained emergency provisions which empowered the Secretary of State for Employment to apply to the National Industrial Relations Court for a "cooling-off" period of sixty days so that he could postpone industrial action where it was likely to injure the national economy or national security. The Secretary of State could also apply for a strike ballot to ensure the union membership supported strike action.

If the Industrial Relations Act was successful, it would break the monopoly position of the trade unions in the labour market, as the Government intended. The Government's objective was not to destroy the trade union movement, or the right to strike, but to engender "responsible" trade unionism, which would use the strike weapon as an ultimate threat, to be used only after due deliberation, rather than the first resort.

The trade unions saw the Act in a somewhat different light. It constituted a direct attack on their ability to protect their members' interests. The Marxist thinkers among the trade union leadership saw the Act in an even broader perspective, as an attempt by the State to promote the interest of the owners of capital against labour by breaking the power of organised labour. So the battle over the Industrial Relations Act was joined. It became law in August 1971. The Annual Congress of the T.U.C. held in September voted to instruct its members not to register under the Act by a majority of 5·6 million to 4·5 million, so that the Government had to attempt to enforce the Act without the consent of those to whom it applied.

The Government's first serious attempt to use the emergency

provisions of the Act was to avert a national railwaymen's strike. The railway unions had submitted a pay demand in excess of the Government's ceiling under its "N-1" policy, which at that time was 8 per cent. The Government, which was the railwaymen's employer through British Railways, applied to the National Industrial Relations Court for a conciliation pause of sixty days, and when this expired the government applied for a secret ballot of the railwaymen on whether to accept an offer advised by an outside arbitrator. The result was an ignominious defeat for the Government – the men rejected the offer by a 5–1 majority. Eventually a settlement for a 13 per cent increase was agreed.

1971 had been the worst year since the War for strikes. Over 13½ million working days had been lost through strikes, 2½ million more than in 1970, the previous worst year.

Early 1972 saw an escalation of the unrest. The National Union of Mineworkers called a strike in January for increases of £9 per week for underground workers, and £8 per week for surface workers. The Government's pay limit at the time would have permitted a pay increase of up to only £1.50 per week. The miners used flying pickets to prevent stocks and fuel and other essential commodities from entering power stations, and to prevent the import of fuel from overseas into British ports. On February 10th, the Government declared a State of Emergency for the second time in its brief period in office. Power cuts were imposed on particular areas on a rota system, and factories had to lay off thousands of workers. There were violent clashes between the pickets and lorries trying to get through to the Saltley Coke depot, with the police getting drawn into the clashes while trying to keep the peace. Eventually, to avert possible tragedy, the depot was closed to all except vehicles carrying trade union permits to collect coke for essential uses such as in hospitals and schools.

In the wake of Saltley, the Government appointed a Court of Inquiry under Lord Wilberforce in an attempt to break the deadlock. The Wilberforce Commission recommended a £6 a week increase for underground workers, which represented a 27 per cent increase over the existing level of wages. The Government, as the miners' employer and the authority which had appointed the Wilberforce Commission, was obliged to accept its recommendation. The strike ended on February 25th. It had destroyed the "N-I" pay policy.

The destruction of the Industrial Relations Act occurred not long afterwards. Dockers in British ports demanded that the loading and unloading of containers should be the prerogative of members of the Transport and General Workers Union. This attempt to establish a closed shop was resisted by other unions, particularly the Union of Shop, Distributive and Allied Workers. In March 1972, dockers began to black lorries delivering goods from container firms, in an effort to secure recognition for the T.G.W.U. A Lancashire firm, Heatons, applied to the National Industrial Relations Court for an injunction requiring the T.G.W.U. to restrain its members from blacking the firm's container lorries, but the union did not recognise the Court and refused to be represented at the hearings. The T.G.W.U. was fined a total of £55,000 for contempt of Court, and the Court also upheld Heatons' application for an injunction against it.

The Transport and General Workers Union pleaded that it could not comply with the injunction because the action was unofficial, so it had no power to force its members to co-operate. This plea was upheld on appeal. The Court then ordered the shop stewards responsible for organising the blacking to appear before it. They refused to do so. On July 25th, five shop stewards were committed to Pentonville Prison for contempt, and entered trade union martyrology as the "Pentonville Five".

The strike spread, and the T.U.C. General Council voted to call a one-day national strike unless the men were released. A national strike was avoided fortuitously as a result of a judgement on July 26th on an appeal to the House of Lords over the original Heatons' case. The Law Lords ruled that trade unions were responsible for the actions of their shop stewards. The Transport and General Workers Union was ordered to pay the previously quashed fines of £55,000 plus the costs of the appeal, a further £25,000; and the five shop stewards were released from Pentonville Prison.

But the damage was already done. The messy strife over the dockers' dispute had brought home to trade unions, in a far more effective way than the arguments of the Marxist militants in their ranks, that the Industrial Relations Act was an instrument which would be used by Government against the interests of organised labour, and was not a neutral arbiter between management and labour.

The remaining trade unions still registered under the Act then deregistered. In the face of this massive opposition, both Government and private sector employers would be reluctant to invoke the provisions of the Act again. In effect, the Act went into abeyance. The warning of the Donovan Commission – that the use of the law in the field of industrial relations would have no positive impact on industrial relations, but merely bring the law itself into disrepute – had proved all too accurate. The Wilson Government had abandoned its attempts to reform industrial relations in response to the pressure within its own ranks. The Heath Government, immune to such internal pressure from the trade union movement, had fought what amounted to a pitched battle with the trade unions in the open field of British industry, and had been forced to concede. Altogether nearly 24 million working days were lost through strikes in 1972, of which 12½ million working days were lost in the first quarter of the year from January to March alone, mainly as a result of the coal and docks strikes.

With his industrial relations strategy in tatters, Edward Heath concentrated during 1972 on pushing to a conclusion the major achievement for which his administration will be remembered. This was Britain's entry into the European Economic Community.

British membership of the Common Market was a major source of political controversy in Britain in the early 1970s. However, the likely economic consequences of British membership for good or ill were usually grossly exaggerated by the protagonists in the Common Market debate. The truth was that the likely effects of membership on Britain's economy were of peripheral importance.

Membership of a customs union such as the European Economic Community entails the elimination of tariff and other barriers to trade between the member countries. Because there are no man-made restrictions on free trade, whether of goods, services, or labour, the members of a customs union share a "common market".

When Britain joined the European Common Market, therefore, it was committed to the progressive reduction of tariff barriers between itself and the other member countries of Western Europe, in return for a reciprocal reduction by those countries. The initial impact of membership on the British economy was thus similar to a devaluation of sterling, insofar as it made British exports to other members of the Common Market cheaper. It consequently opened up opportunities for an increase in the volume of exports from Britain to the rest of Western Europe. However, membership of the

Common Market was dissimilar from a currency devaluation in that, whereas devaluation of the £ sterling would make the price of imports from abroad more expensive in terms of sterling, joining the Common Market and reducing tariff barriers to imports from the Common Market made the price of those imports cheaper.

For this reason, entry into the Common Market was far riskier for Britain than was devaluation. The economic case for entry was essentially that the risks were more than outweighed by the potential benefits in terms of export opportunities for Britain in the Common Market. However, the ability of Britain to seize the opportunities offered by membership rested on the same factors as her ability to make a success of devaluation: notably, the capacity of the economy to grow and adapt in response to the new trading situation. That is to say, the prospect for success rested on the speed with which the British economy could reallocate its resources from the sectors in which it was comparatively uncompetitive, and into the sectors in which it was comparatively competitive, so that it would complement the economies of Western Europe.

The slow rate of adaptability and growth of the British economy had been the fundamental reason for Britain's decline in the world economy since the Second World War. Non-membership of the European Common Markert was incidental. Other capitalist economies such as those of Japan, Switzerland and the Scandinavian countries achieved much faster rates of growth of real income than Britain outside major customs unions. Britain's entry into the European Economic Community in 1972 would not itself improve the underlying rate of growth of the British economy. What it would do was offer great potential benefits if Britain herself could solve her fundamental problems.

Nineteen seventy-two could have been the year when the Heath Government began to address itself to this issue. With its attempts to reform the workings of the labour market destroyed, the Government could have undertaken a reappraisal of the assumptions on which its economic policy was based. It failed to do so. Instead of examining the proposition that distortions in the labour market lay at the heart of Britain's related problems of inflation and slow growth, the Heath Government took this premise as given.

Ironically enough, this premise led the Heath Government to adopt the very instrument of which it had been so critical when it had been applied by the 1964–70 Labour Government: the instrument of incomes policy. In November 1972, the Government introduced Stage One of a statutory incomes policy, comprising a complete freeze on all wages and prices for ninety days. This was followed in 1973 by Stage Two, which allowed pay increases of £1 plus 4 per cent. The actual increase in earnings under the policy was much greater than this, mainly because increases in pay which were in line with the policy were allowable as unavoidable costs which could be passed on by firms in higher prices, and this left very little leeway for price rises caused by increases in the costs of other inputs, particularly imports. Yet the price of imports had been given a sharp upward kick by influences outside the incomes policy. The collapse of the U.S. dollar and the Bretton Woods system of fixed exchange rates in 1972 and the floating of sterling had resulted in an upsurge in the costs of imports. In the twelve months between November 1972 and October 1973, the prices of industry's basic raw materials rose by over 40 per cent, a reflection of the international boom in the dollar prices of basic commodities.

Further, the nature of the Stage Two norm – based on a flat £1 per week, plus 4 per cent, and subject to a maximum of £250 p.a., irrespective of the initial wage of the worker – was bound to squeeze differentials and distort the workings of the labour market.

It was in recognition of this, and in order to correct the anomalies in the pay structure that had developed in the previous three years, that Stage Three of the Heath Government's incomes policy included a greater element of flexibility. The norm for pay increases was set at £2.25 per week or 7 per cent, whichever was larger. A 1 per cent "flexibility margin" over and above this norm was allowed for groups which could show that they had fallen behind comparable groups of workers as a consequence of past pay policies. Stage Three also included provisions for extra pay for those who had to work unsocial hours. But its major innovation was in the introduction of threshold payments of 40p per week for every increase of 1 per cent in the retail price index (the official measure of the cost of living) above 6 per cent. The intention of threshold payments was to provide automatic adjustments in wages to compensate for inflation, so that the attempts of trade unions to get sufficient increases in pay to cover future anticipated price rises would not themselves become an independent cause of those price rises, when passed on by the employers.

In October 1973, the National Coal Board had offered the miners a package which made full use of the provisions of Stage Three. The package comprised the 7 per cent norm permissible, plus 1 per cent holiday pay, plus 4·3 per cent for unsocial hours on nightshift, plus 0·7 per cent for odds and ends, and finally 3·5 per cent if the miners' accepted the National Coal Board's productivity scheme, adding up to a total offer of 16½ per cent. The Coal Board probably made a tactical mistake in making this offer, which was the maximum possible offer it could make under Stage Three, as its first offer. To justify their existence, trade union officials are almost forced to reject the first offer in order to demonstrate that they are getting a better deal for their members than they would have obtained without bargaining. The National Union of Mineworkers duly did reject the N.C.B.'s offer, and launched an overtime ban on November 12th to reduce coal stocks in preparation for a later possible coal strike.

Meanwhile, international events were moving to shift bargaining power decisively in the miners' favour. The Arab oil-producing countries were attempting to use their control of most of the West's oil supplies to put pressure on the West to act against Israel. In October, they had announced a 25 per cent reduction in their supplies of oil to the West, and these reductions were already beginning to bite.

The day after the miners announced their overtime ban, the Government declared a State of Emergency and imposed controls on fuel consumption in Government departments and nationalised industries. A road speed limit of 50 m.p.h. was imposed and petrol coupons were issued at Post Offices in readiness for petrol rationing.

With no concessions on either side, and no prospect of concessions, the Government decided to put British industry on a three-day week as from January 1st, 1974, in an effort to conserve fuel. On the same day, the Arab oil producers increased the price of oil to U.S. $11.65 per barrel, representing nearly a fivefold increase over its price of $2.40 a year earlier.

The increase in oil prices greatly strengthened the hand of the miners, as the producers of coal, which was the major alternative to oil as a source of energy. In view of this, the Trades Union Congress proposed on January 9th that if the Government permitted an exceptional increase to the miners outside the Stage Three guidelines, then other unions would not quote the miners' settlement in support of their own claims. The Government rejected this proposal. In retrospect, it can be seen as the second major tactical error made by the employers' side during the course of the strike.

The next major development in the strike occurred on January 24th, when the Pay Board – the body established by the Government under Stage Two to supervise the implementation of pay increases under the policy – published its relativities report, which revealed that the miners had suffered a loss in their relative wages as a consequence of pay policy, and an exceptional increase might therefore be justified. Still the Government refused to budge.

On February 4th the National Union of Mineworkers balloted its members on an Executive recommendation to strike. The miners voted 81 per cent in favour, and the following day the N.U.M. executive announced the overtime ban would be ended and a full-scale strike begin on February 9th.

In the face of an escalation of the strike, Edward Heath announced on February 7th that the Queen would dissolve Parliament the following day and a General Election would be held on February 28th. The Conservatives went into the election campaign to establish "Who governs the country – the Government or the trade unions?" But one of the leading Conservatives, Enoch Powell, refused to fight on this slogan, arguing that it was a fraudulent one because the Conservatives had been returned in 1970 on a manifesto which rejected statutory incomes policy, and now they were fighting to sustain such a policy.

More generally, the electorate were disillusioned by the politics of confrontation between the Government and organised labour, even though they were far from confident that the Labour Party would perform any better than the Conservatives. On election day, the largest gainers were the third parties, the Liberals in England and the Nationalists in Scotland and Wales. But the Labour Party won just enough votes from the Conservatives to be returned as the largest single party in the House of Commons, and to form a minority Government.

John Grigg, in an analysis of the miners' strike in the *Observer*, concluded that, "Mr Heath is the first British Prime Minister to have been brought down mainly by the political exploitation of industrial power. A big trade union has done to a Tory leader what big business could never have done to a Socialist." This view was not an uncommon one; but the facts permit of different interpretations.

The view that the trade unions were seeking to govern the country, or even to prevent the elected Government from doing so, is hardly tenable. It was the Government itself which set the tone for industrial relations; the trade unions had merely attempted to defend their own and their members' interests. The attempt by the Government to use the force of law, first in its Industrial Relations Act and then in the statutory incomes policy, in a way perceived by trade unionists to be inimical to their interests was bound to provoke resistance. Eventually, when the Government decided it could not concede any more, something had to give. Had the Government won a decisive victory at the February 1974 Election, then the miners would have been forced to concede. As it turned out, it was the Government itself which fell. The arbiter was not a "big trade union", but the electorate itself, which passed judgement on the Heath Government.

III

The incoming Labour Government of 1974 pursued a tentative approach towards the labour market. The Trade Union and Labour Relations Act, 1974, abolished the National Industrial Relations Court and repealed the 1971 Industrial Relations Act. It also extended trade unions' right to picket. Otherwise, it represented little more than a return to the pre-1971 status quo in the labour market.

The Conservative Government's incomes policy was also abandoned and replaced by a "Social Contract" between Government and the trade unions, by which the trade unions agreed voluntarily to restrain their wage demands. This voluntary restraint did not prove effective. Over the period lasting from the beginning of 1974 to August 1975, money earnings in Britain rose by a staggering 40 per cent. Britain appeared to be hurtling towards hyper-inflation as a consequence of the free-for-all in pay bargaining.

It was against this background that the Government won the consent of the T.U.C. for a voluntary restraint of wage increases. The T.U.C. guidelines, endorsed by a Government White Paper entitled "The Attack on Inflation", laid down a maximum for pay increases of £6 per week, with no increases at all for those earning in excess of £8,500 per year.

There were three features of the £6 limit which distinguished it from previous incomes policies. Firstly, it was a flat money amount rather than a flat percentage amount. This implied that it would tend to squeeze differentials, because a £6 pay award would represent a higher proportionate increase, the lower the initial level of a worker's wages. Thus, for someone earning £60 per week, £6 extra represents a 10 per cent increase; whereas for a worker on £120 per week, £6 is only a 5 per cent increase.

The second distinguishing feature of the £6 limit was that it was not a statutory amount laid down by law. Yet in spite of the absence of formal legal backing, the £6 limit had more effective sanctions to support it than any previous incomes policy. In the White Paper, the Government stated that grants and loans to any sector of local government or the nationalised industries paying its employees over the limit might be withheld; while any firm in the private sector which broke the guidelines was liable to have its contracts with Government revoked.

The third feature of the £6 limit was that it was enforced by the trade unions and their members themselves. Thus, the incomes policy was not being enforced on the trade unions by an outside authority, but rather was voluntarily accepted by a conscious decision of the trade unions. This fact is even more impressive because the voluntary restraint occurred against a background of price inflation, and the increase in money wages did not keep pace with the increase in retail prices. For the first time ever in peacetime, the industrial work-force as a whole accepted a voluntary cut in their real wages.

The passage of the 1975 Employment Protection Act was an important element in securing the trade unions' co-operation for wage restraint. The Act considerably strengthened the rights of trade unions. A trade union could obtain recognition from an employer as the official negotiating body for his workers, and negotiate an agreement for a closed shop. Should the employer decline to reach such an agreement, the union could appeal through the Advisory, Conciliation and Arbitration Service (A.C.A.S.), which had been established the previous year, for an award of recognition. The Employment Protection Act also protected employees from dismissal for joining a trade union, and required employers to consult with representatives of the trade unions concerned before making any members of those unions redundant.

The effect of the 1975 Act was to formalise many de facto rights of trade unions, rather than giving them any completely new rights. In this, it was following one of the central recommendations of the Donovan Commission: that is, the formalisation of the "custom and practice" of industrial relations. The Act proved reasonably successful, although the difficulty of enforcing recognition of a trade union on an employer was illustrated in the long drawn out and bitter Grunwick dispute of 1976.

The comparatively successful alliance between Government and organised labour continued in the 1976–77 pay round. A Special Congress of the T.U.C., held in June 1976, approved a further year of wage restraint by a majority of nine million votes to half a million – a 95 per cent majority. The guidelines comprised a 5 per cent norm for pay increases, subject to a minimum increase of £2.50 per week and a maximum of £4 per week. These limits, like the flat-rate increase of the year before, tended to improve the relative position of the low paid. As a quid pro quo for the unions' support, the Government further extended the legal rights of the trade unions in the 1976 Trade Union and Labour Relations (Amendment) Act. Over the two pay rounds 1975–77, real wages fell by some 5 per cent. The annual rate of inflation also fell from 24 per cent during 1974 to only 8 per cent during 1978.

However, after two years of voluntary wage restraint, the trade unions felt they had done their share towards the reduction of the rate of inflation, and were eager to restore the process of free collective bargaining which was their reason for existence. The Government, on the other hand, was keen to maintain pay restraint and not lose the fruits of the previous two years. Restraint was continued during the 1977–78 pay round, when a maximum of 10 per cent was supported by the threat of sanctions against employers who paid more, in the form of the withdrawal of Government contracts from firms which paid over the limit. The policy was still not statutory, but was intended to be enforced by the voluntary compliance of one of the parties to the collective bargaining process; in this case, the relevant party was the employers rather than the work-force. Because the policy was not statutory, the Government did not run the risk of coming into direct conflict with a trade union breaking the guidelines, as the Heath Government had.

However, by the end of the 1977–78 pay round the strains of three successive years of pay restraint and the distortion of differentials that they had caused were becoming irresistible. The Prime

Minister, James Callaghan (who had succeeded Harold Wilson on his retirement in March 1976), addressed the T.U.C. in July 1978 on the subject of pay policy. His speech was listened to, in the words of one trade union leader, "like an old wives' tale on the ears of a drowsy man". The *Economist* magazine of July 22nd, 1978, commented: "When the T.U.C. leaders stayed at Downing Street for a drink afterwards, only Mr Clive Jenkins, the boss of ASTMS, the white collar union, did the round of the cocktail-sippers breathing fire and brimstone. As usual, nobody took much notice of him." Perhaps it was this apathy that induced James Callaghan to ignore the danger-signals and make the fateful decision to try to get through another winter of pay restraint before calling a General Election.

The 5 per cent limit on pay increases proposed by the Callaghan Government for the 1978–79 pay round was never on. In November the Ford car workers set the pace for wage increases when they settled for a 17 per cent increase after a nine-week strike. After that, the floodgates were open. By the end of the year, the norm for pay increases was running at 15 per cent and industrial unrest was back to the proportions of the Heath years.

1979 was to prove the worst since the Second World War in terms of working days lost through strikes. A total of 29 million working days were lost, five million more than even in the disastrous year of 1972.

The crumbling of the Labour Government's labour market policy undermined the basis of its authority. The Labour Party's narrow electoral victories in 1974 had been won on the platform that it could work better with the trade unions than the Conservatives. The Winter of Discontent of 1978–79 effectively destroyed this platform. The Labour Government lost a vote of confidence in the Commons in April 1979, and duly went on to lose the General Election in May. The Conservative Party was returned to office with a clear majority of 55 seats over all other parties. Thus three successive Governments had been defeated at the polls, in 1970, 1974 and 1979, following the failure of their labour market policies.

The instruments and stated objectives of the labour market policies of the 1965–79 period had been essentially twofold.

Firstly, reform of the legal framework in which collective bargaining took place was intended to reduce the incidence of strikes and bring about a more "responsible" form of trade unionism. In fact, the number of working days lost through strikes – which, as the Donovan Commission had pointed out, had not been particularly high by international standards before 1968 – increased from an average of less than 3 million each year in the period 1946–67 to more than 10½ million per year in the period since 1968. The upsurge in industrial unrest in the period 1968–72 was a direct response to Government's attempts to impose reform in collective bargaining procedures from outside. After the defeat of the Industrial Relations Act in 1972, the number of working days lost through strikes fell back until 1978–79, but not to its pre-1968 level. The story of failure is shown graphically in Figure I.

The message was that, as the Donovan Commission recommended, the role of law in respect of collective bargaining should be a passive one, giving legal form to the consensus already existing within industry as to what subjects should be covered by collective bargaining and what procedures should be followed. The law should not attempt to impose the subject-matter and procedures on the parties to collective bargaining from the outside. If it does attempt to do so, it will be flouted.

At the time of writing, it is still not clear whether this message has got through to Britain's policy-makers.

The second main instrument of Government intervention in the labour market was incomes policy. The stated aim of incomes policy was to bring the increase in money wages into line with the increase in output produced, thereby reducing the rate of inflation and making the British economy more competitive internationally. A subsidiary aim of incomes policy was the more equitable distribution of income between wage-earners.

Evaluated against these objectives, incomes policy, like the attempts at legal reform of industrial relations, was an unmitigated failure. During the period since the mid-1960s, the rate of increase in money wages has accelerated, while the rate of growth of industrial production has declined. Consequently, the growth of real wages, which averaged nearly 2½ per cent per annum in the period 1946–67, has fallen to an average of less than 1 per cent in the years since 1968. The increase in money wages has been insufficient to do more than just offset the increase in retail prices, which has also accelerated since the mid-1960s. Only for one brief period, in 1975–78, was incomes policy applied with success, and contributed towards a falling rate of price inflation.

Figure I

THE STRUGGLE IN THE LABOUR MARKET
WORKING DAYS LOST THROUGH STRIKES, 1946–1981

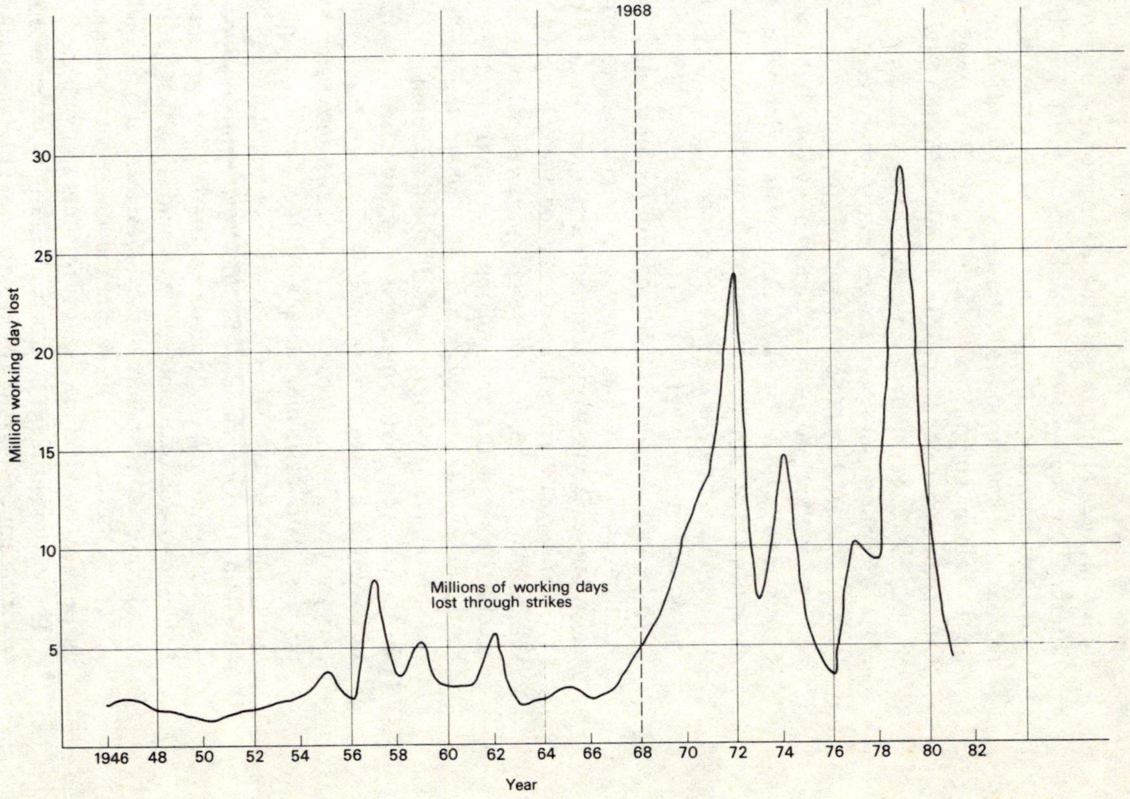

Nevertheless, in spite of this poor record, incomes policy still has its supporters. They argue that, for an incomes policy to be successful, it must fulfil certain criteria. Its failure has, they maintain, been attributable to the absence of one or more of these criteria. To be *enforceable*, two conditions must hold. Firstly, the guidelines laid down by the incomes policy must be clear and realistic. If the norm or maximum set down by the incomes policy is too low, then the policy will simply be evaded, as was that of the Callaghan Government in 1978–79, and the Wilson Government in the late 1960s. Secondly, the policy must be sufficiently flexible to allow exceptions for special cases. But if the exceptions are too broadly drawn, then the norms will lose their meaning, as they did because of the "productivity deals" allowable under the Wilson Government's 1966–70 policy. Conversely, if the policy allows no exceptions at all, then once even one group breaches it, the whole policy will crumble, as the Heath Government's policy did when it was broken by the miners in 1974.

To be *enforced*, two further conditions must hold. The policy must have adequate machinery to administer it, to monitor any exceptions to it, and to make recommendations for its reform. And this administrative machinery must be backed up by sanctions sufficient to enforce it. Where the incomes policy is voluntarily accepted by both the trade unions and employers, these sanctions need not be particularly strong. But where the guidelines are strongly opposed by both organised labour and employers, then any sanctions, even those supported by statute, are not likely to be successful in enforcing the policy.

In the years since 1966, Britain has seen a succession of incomes policies. The particular details of the policies of the Wilson Government of 1964–70, the Heath Government of 1970–74, and the Callaghan Government of 1976–79 were quite distinct. Yet each ended in failure and electoral defeat for the Government.

The advocates of incomes policy would argue that this failure was in each case a consequence of the failure to apply one or more of the essential criteria for a successful incomes policy, compounded by the political errors made by Governments applying them.

There is an old adage that "a bad workman blames his tools". But when the same tools fail to produce the required results in the hands of several different workmen, the question arises – is the fault that of the workmen or rather that of the tools themselves? Perhaps the reason for the failure of successive incomes policies was not merely their technical faults, compounded by mistakes made by particular politicians at different times; perhaps the reason for their failure was that they were the wrong tools, used because of a fundamental misapprehension of the nature of the task to which they were applied.

And perhaps the consequence of tinkering with the delicate machinery of the British economy with inappropriate tools was merely to cause worse distortions and frictions than would have occurred had it been left alone altogether.

And perhaps the upsurge in industrial unrest and money wages after 1968 was largely the consequence of these distortions and frictions.

If this is so, then it is time to examine the assumptions on which incomes policy was based.

IV

The fundamental assumption on which the case for incomes policy rested was that inflation was a uniquely *British* problem, and its causes lay in the particular structure of the British labour market.

This argument was put by Aubrey Jones, who had been the chairman of the 1964–70 Wilson Government's Prices and Incomes Board, in his book *The New Inflation*. What was "new" about price inflation in post-war Britain, according to Jones, was that it arose in consequence of trade union pressure rather than excess monetary demand. Jones argued that at full employment level, trade unions in rapidly growing sectors of the economy were able to secure large wage increases for their members, which were subsequently transmitted through the economy, because trade unions in other sectors of the economy demanded corresponding increases in their own members' wages. The employers in these other sectors were not able to absorb these wage increases by improvements in productivity, and so were forced to pass on the increases to the consumer in the form of higher prices. In the words of Harold Wilson, one man's wage increase became another man's price increase. Higher money wages thus did not result in improvements in living-standards but merely in higher retail prices.

Once this process started, there was no mechanism to prevent it from continuing. If the Government was committed to maintaining full employment of labour, as it was in Britain until the early 1970s, then the threat that excessive wage increases would price workers out of a job was not very strong. Instead, trade unions would react to higher prices by trying to secure still higher money wages for their members. And this started another cycle of the "wage-price" spiral.

The only way to stop the wage-price spiral from continuing in an ever upward direction, according to Jones, was to intervene in it directly, by holding down wage increases to the level justifiable by improvements in productivity. An incomes policy was the instrument for doing this.

If this diagnosis was correct, then the prescription of incomes policy might have met with more success than in fact it did. But the evidence to support the thesis that upward pressure on wage costs was the primary reason for inflation in post-war Britain is less than convincing.

Aubrey Jones' own notion that there was wage leadership by the fastest-growing sectors of the economy is not borne out by the facts. There has been no correlation between changes in aggregate wages and changes in productivity in the fastest-growing sectors. Nor have attempts to correlate some measure of labour "militancy" with the rate of increase in retail prices met with success. Aubrey Jones himself claimed to find a relationship between the number of working days lost through strikes and the rise in retail prices between 1967 and 1973. But this relationship does not exist for either the 1946–66 period or for the years since 1973. Nor has there been any significant correlation between other proxies of labour militancy, such as the numbers of workers involved in strikes or the proportion of the work-force which is unionised, and either the level or the rate of change in the retail price index.

The acid test of whether a wage-push inflation exists is the relative shares of wages and profits in national income. In aggregate, an independent upward pressure on wages should result in an increase in the share of wages in national income and a fall in the share of profits. In fact, the share of wages in national income in the United Kingdom has fallen since the Second World War, from nearly 50 per cent in 1946 to only 40 per cent by the end of the 1960s. The share of the gross trading profits of private companies and statutory corporations fluctuated between 18½ per cent and 21 per cent of net national income between 1951 and 1973. It showed a slight secular decline, but the extent of this decline was nothing like enough to bear out the "cost-push" thesis. Only in the 1973–75 period did the share of gross trading profits in national income drop sharply in a way that would suggest aggressive upward pressure from costs. The share of national income which has been growing most rapidly since World War Two, at the expense mainly of wages and incomes from self-employment rather than trading profits, has been salaries. The share of salaries in national income, which was less than one-quarter at the end of the Second World War, rose to well over one-third by the end of the 1970s. This reflects, not aggressive upward pressure by salary-earners, but rather the growth of the proportion of salaried white-collar workers in the total labour force, which has been concomitant with the growth of the service sector (including Government, banking and insurance, and higher education) in the economy.

The evidence indicates that the single most important cause of inflation in post-war Britain was not pressures on costs, but rather an excess of monetary demand over the supply of goods. Excessive monetary demand simultaneously pulled up the prices of goods and of the labour employed to produce those goods.

Inflation in Britain since the Second World War can be divided into two distinct phases, and the year of 1968 is the watershed. Before 1968, the rate of inflation averaged 4 per cent p.a. Immediately after the War, there was a release of pent-up demand following the gradual easing of wartime controls on spending. The once-off impact of this release on prices had tapered off by the end of the 1940s. However, it was succeeded in the early 1950s by a sharp increase in the prices of imports at the time of an international commodity price boom. In 1951 and 1952, retail prices rose by more than 9 per cent p.a. After the Korean War, the increase in commodity prices ended. Between 1953 and 1967, the rise in retail prices never exceeded 5 per cent in any calendar year, and the average rate of increase was around 3 per cent per annum.

The second phase of post-war inflation began after 1968, when the rate of inflation steadily accelerated from 5 per cent to a peak of nearly 30 per cent in 1974. Between 1974 and 1978, the rate of inflation was slowly brought down; after the winter of 1978–79 it began to rise again. The average rate of inflation in the years from 1969 to 1979 was more than 13 per cent, and on a rising trend.

In 1958 Professor A. W. Phillips published a paper on "Unemployment and Money Wage Rates" in *Economica*. In this paper

Phillips identified a statistical relationship between the rate of change of money wage rates and the level of unemployment in the United Kingdom. The relationship that Phillips had identified became known as the "Phillips Curve", and it showed that the rate of change of money wage rates had historically been inversely correlated with the level of unemployment – that is, the greater the level of unemployment, the lower the increase in money wage rates, and vice versa.

What the Phillips Curve showed was not a functional relationship between two variables, but rather two effects of the same cause, which was the level of monetary demand, and fluctuations in it. As monetary demand increased – whether from an upswing in activity in the private sector in the course of the trade cycle, or from an increase in net government spending, or from a combination of the two – so firms increased the sales of their goods. They could meet this increase by running down stocks for a short period, but if it continued they would have to expand production. This required the employment of more workers. Firms employed more workers by drawing on the pool of unemployed workers and by raising wage rates to attract workers from other firms. At the same time, they might take advantage of buoyant demand by raising the prices at which they sold their goods, which would increase their profits. Conversely, if monetary demand was falling, firms would both lay off some of their work-force (or not replace workers who leave or retire) and be less willing to increase the wage rates of the workers who remain, because they would not be in a good position to raise their prices.

After 1967, the Phillips Curve in its original form began to break down, and both wage rates and the level of unemployment increased simultaneously. The proximate reason for this was an acceleration in the rate of inflation. The Phillips Curve, as originally specified, showed the relationship between a monetary variable – wage rates – and a real variable – unemployment. This relationship would only hold if the real value of money was itself not changing, or was not perceived as changing by workers. If workers and their trade union representatives believed that the value of money was being reduced by inflation, then past inflation and expected future inflation would become a significant factor in the determination of money wage rates. To maintain the real value of money wage rates it would be necessary that these rates increase in at least the same proportion as the level of retail prices. There was thus a different trade-off between money wage rates and the level of unemployment for every different rate of inflation.

There were other factors in the breakdown of the Phillips Curve. Firstly, wage rates became less reliable as a guide to actual earnings because of the growth of wage drift at plant level to avoid the attempts at regulation of the labour market by Government. So wage rates reflected fluctuations in the demand for labour less well than the actual earnings negotiated by shop stewards in the "unofficial" labour market. A second factor was improvements in the level of unemployment benefit in the mid-1960s, which reduced the cost of unemployment relative to being in a job. Unemployment benefit was less than half of average wages in Britain in the 1950–66 period, but after the introduction of the earnings-related supplement by the 1964–70 Labour Government, the ratio of unemployment benefit to the wages of an average employed worker rose to over two-thirds. This increase could be expected to make unemployed workers more selective about the type of jobs they accepted, and prepared to spend more time searching for employment, and this would cause a one-off upward shift in the Phillips Curve. That is, it would result in an increase in the level of unemployment associated with any given change in wage rates.

However, factors such as these are very much of secondary importance. Overwhelmingly the most important factor in the destruction of the Phillips Relation was the acceleration in the rate of inflation which occurred in Britain between 1967 and 1974.

The "cost-push" explanation of this acceleration in inflation fails to explain why it was an international phenomenon. It is true that there was an increase in labour unrest and the level of wage demands throughout Western Europe in the late 1960s, led by France in 1968, and followed by West Germany, Italy, and Britain in 1969. But this unrest was largely an attempt to *maintain* real wages in the face of price inflation, rather than to increase real wages.

The growth of world money supply offers a better explanation for the international nature of inflation. This growth was stimulated by a succession of large deficits on the Balance of Payments of the largest of capitalist economies, the United States of America. In the late 1960s and early 1970s, the U.S.A. Balance of Payments on the current account were as follows:

Year	*U.S.A. Payments deficit ($ million)*
1965	−1335
1966	−1357
1967	−3571
1968	171
1969	−7012
1970	−4715
1971	−22,719
1972	−14,684

These payments deficits represented an outflow of dollars from the U.S.A., because American spending on imports exceeded earnings in foreign exchange from exports, and there was thus a large net addition in the numbers of dollars on the money markets of the world. The U.S. dollar had been the most important trading currency of the western world since the Second World War, so that an increase in the volume of dollars represented an expansion in the world's money supply. Furthermore, the development of the Euro-dollar market meant that the extra dollars were transmitted rapidly into international trading activity, with the consequence that there was a sharp increase in international monetary demand in the late 1960s.

An expansion of monetary demand can be met by a corresponding increase in output. However, if productive resources are fully employed, then such an increase in output cannot occur. In this case, an expansion of monetary demand must result, after a lag of between 18 months and three years, in a rise in prices.

This is exactly what happened. The I.M.F.'s figures on world prices since the Second World War show that after twenty years of secular decline in commodity prices, there was a sudden upsurge during the 1972–74 period. Between the beginning of 1972 and the end of 1974, the I.M.F.'s index of world commodity prices rose by well over 100 per cent. More generally, world consumer prices over the same period rose by around one-third.

The upsurge in the world's money supply in 1970–72 was directly related to the U.S.A.'s Payments deficits in those years, which led to the collapse of the U.S. dollar in November 1971 because the supply of dollars to world markets persistently exceeded the demand for them to pay for American exports.

The functional relationship between world money supply and prices is shown on the scatter diagram in Figure II. The rate of inflation, on the vertical axis, is regressed against the rate of increase in world money supply two years earlier, on the horizontal axis. The graph shows a clear relationship between world inflation and monetary growth.

The scatter diagram brings out two other points worthy of note. Firstly, the largest deviation from the trend line occurred in 1974, the year the O.P.E.C. countries quadrupled the price at which they were prepared to sell oil. The actual rate of world inflation in this year was over 15 per cent, compared to a rate of around 10 per cent which would have been predicted by reference to the trend line alone. This difference can be attributed to upward pressure on costs, particularly the costs of fuel. Secondly, the correlation between the rate of inflation and the change in world money supply two years earlier is high, but not perfect. In particular, it will be noted that at low rates of inflation, the actual rates of inflation mostly lie below those which would be predicted by reference to the trend line alone; while at rates of inflation greater than about 8 per cent they mostly lie above the trend. What this suggests is that the best line that could be drawn to fit the various points would not be a straight line, but a curve, the slope of which would gradually increase as the rate of growth of the money supply increased. A straight-line relationship would exist only if the rate at which money was spent – the "velocity of circulation" of money – remained constant as the rate of inflation increased. In fact, the evidence is that the velocity of circulation tends to increase with the rate of inflation and the nominal rate of interest. The reason is that as the rate of inflation increases, so does the rate at which the purchasing power of money falls, and consequently individuals have an incentive to hold as little of their wealth in the form of money as possible.

The growth in money supply and the increase in the rate at which that money was spent can explain the international acceleration in inflation which occurred in the late 1960s and early 1970s. The single most important factor in the growth of the world's money supply was the Balance of Payments deficit of the U.S.A., which was the result of excessive monetary demand within the U.S.A. itself, so that more imports were drawn in to the country. The cause of this excessive monetary demand was American Government Budget deficits, incurred largely because of the sharp increase in American

Figure II

MONEY SUPPLY AND INFLATION IN NON-COMMUNIST COUNTRIES, 1952–1980

(Source: I.M.F. Survey, November 12th, 1979)

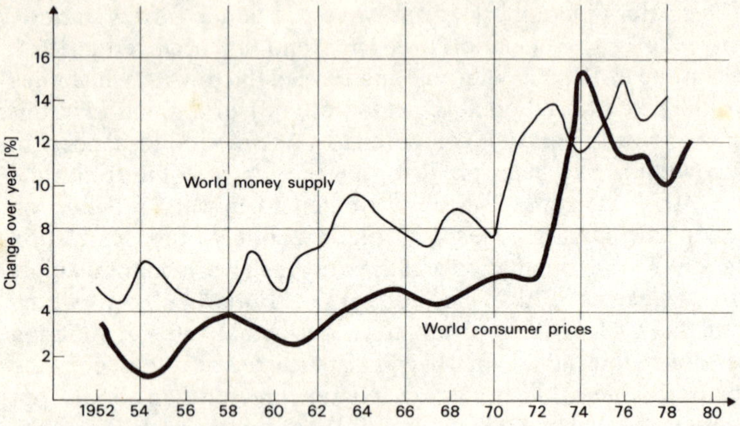

RELATIONSHIP BETWEEN THE INTERNATIONAL RATE OF INFLATION AND THE RATE OF GROWTH OF WORLD MONEY SUPPLY

(Source: I.M.F. Survey, November 1979)

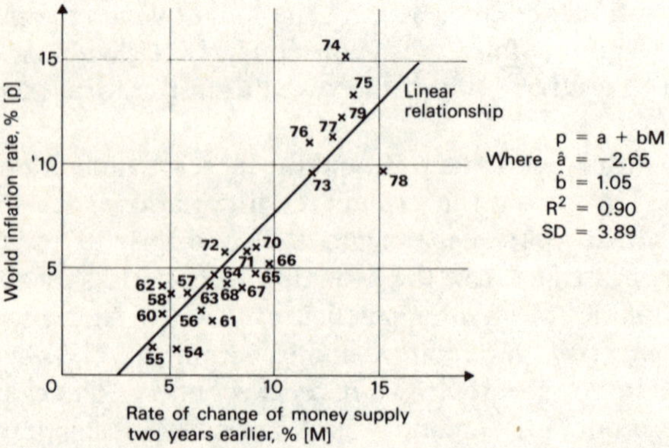

military expenditure required to execute the Vietnam War.

In this, the international monetary inflation of the late 1960s and early 1970s had similar origins to past inflations. As one of the most articulate of contemporary economic commentators, Samuel Brittan, put it, "Since the Roman Empire, military expenditure has been the greatest force both for the enslavement of the individual to the State – and for currency debasement." ("Guns and Big Government", *Financial Times*, 28.1.80.) Brittan's association between increase in military expenditure and debasement of the currency through inflation has been borne out by the historical experience of the United Kingdom since the Industrial Revolution. The three major inflations in the U.K. in the two centuries before the late 1960s each coincided with periods of major wars – the Napoleonic Wars in the early nineteenth century, and the First and Second World Wars during the first half of the twentieth century. On each occasion, there were discontinuous jumps in Government expenditure to finance the execution of the war. And on each occasion Government revenue rose more slowly than expenditure, and the gap was filled by deficit financing and increases in the size of the National Debt, which in turn generated sharp price inflations. Inflation in wartime acted as a tax on income earners by reducing the real value of their income, while the government expenditure which caused it mobilised resources for the needs of war.

What was different about the post-1967 inflation was that it was caused by military expenditure for a war in which Britain was not an active combatant. The "inflation tax" was being levied on the British worker to fund expenditure for a purpose which was no concern of his. In view of this, it is not surprising that he attempted to resist the tax, and to maintain his real income.

The British Government of the late 1960s and early 1970s completely misread the nature and causes of the inflationary problem. They interpreted it as a "cost push" rather than a monetary inflation – and acted accordingly to cut the increases in costs, and particularly in wages. This generated confrontation between the Government on the one hand, and the trade unions seeking to protect their members' living-standards on the other. This avoidable confrontation worsened both the inflationary process and the level of industrial unrest in Britain.

In a pamphlet entitled *Do trade unions cause inflation?* Turner, Jackson and Wilkinson distinguished between "normal inflation", of around 3–5 per cent p.a., in which conflict is over the distribution of the increments to a growing national income, rather than over the basic distribution of income between different groups; and "strato-inflation" of 30 per cent and over, where conflict is no longer over the incremental income, but over the basic distribution of national income between competing social classes. They argued that whereas inflation in the developed western democracies was normal, in Latin America it had been of the "strato" type.

By the early 1970s, Britain was poised uncomfortably between the two rates; her rate of inflation lay above 5 per cent but below 30 per cent. The inflationary process was no longer normal, but well on the way to becoming highly political. In the campaigns against the Industrial Relations Act and in the two miners' strikes of 1972 and 1973–74, the actions of organised labour were not motivated by purely economic ends, but had political overtones. The sharp profits squeeze in 1973–75 was caused by upward pressure on costs in a depressed market – and this upward pressure was the consequence of increases in the prices of imported commodities, particularly oil, and also of resistance by organised labour to what they perceived as attempts to reduce their real wages.

The success of incomes policy in the years 1975–77 was primarily because, for the first time, incomes policy was a relevant policy instrument, addressed to one of the causes of Britain's inflation. That cause was upward pressure on money wages; but ironically, this upward pressure had arisen partly in reaction against previous incomes policies. The major cause of inflation in Britain other than this brief period in the mid-1970s had not been aggressive upward pressure on wages. The major cause had been an excess in the rate of growth of monetary demand over the rate of growth of real output. Furthermore, excessive monetary demand was not an exclusively British problem, but an international phenomenon affecting all the western economies during the period after 1967.

Chapter Three

THE NEW ORTHODOXY

They wonder much to hear that gold, which in itself is so useless a thing, should be everywhere so much esteemed, that even men for whom it was made, and by whom it has its value, should yet be thought less than it is.

Sir Thomas More, *Utopia*

I

IN 1968 a comparatively minor Conservative politician was catapulted to national prominence.

His name was Enoch Powell, and the issue which catapulted him to prominence was that of race.

It also led to his eviction from the Conservative Shadow Cabinet. On the day after his first melodramatic speech on the subject of race at Birmingham on April 21st, 1968, he was sacked by the Conservative leader, Edward Heath. He was never again to hold office, either in Government or in Opposition. Yet he remained one of the most influential figures in British politics for the next decade.

Powell struck a responsive chord among a large section of the British people. Like all successful demagogues, he played not on their hopes or ideals, but on their fear of the unknown, of things they did not comprehend.

The fear was that Britain would become swamped by immigrants from the New Commonwealth: the newly independent African, Asian and Caribbean states which had formerly been colonies of the British Empire. According to Powell, the size of the immigrant population in 1968 was some one and a quarter million people, and he calculated that on the current trends it would increase to four and a half million by the year 2000, when immigrants would comprise 6 per cent of the total population. But the immigration "problem", argued Powell, did not derive from sheer numbers.

The very growth in numbers would increase the already

> striking fact of dense geographical concentration, so that the urban parts of whole towns and cities in Yorkshire, the Midlands, and the Home Counties would be preponderantly or exclusively Afro-Asian in population. There would be several Washingtons in England. From these whole areas the indigenous population, the people of England, who fondly imagine that this is their country and these are their home towns, would have been dislodged . . . I do not believe it is in human nature that a country, and a country such as ours, should passively watch the transformation of whole areas which lie at the heart of it into alien territory.
>
> (Enoch Powell speaking at Eastbourne, November 1968)

The solution Powell offered to "passively watching" this "transformation into alien territory" was twofold. Firstly, a total and immediate halt to all coloured immigration into Britain, extending not only to new workers but also to the wives and children seeking to join those who had already arrived. And secondly, a "voluntary but organised, financed, and subsidised repatriation of Commonwealth immigrants, preferably under a new Ministry of Repatriation".

Had Powell's assumptions of the question of immigration been correct, then his proposed solutions might have made some sense, since few faulted his logic. His assumptions, which come out clearly in his speech, were essentially that the immigrants were "alien" and could never successfully integrate, and that they would continue to come into Britain in increasing numbers unless physically prevented from doing so.

These assumptions ignored the possibility that the immigrants were capable of communicating with, understanding, and sympathising with other human beings, if only they were given the chance. And in Britain, they were given the chance, although not as much chance as the indigenous population. There was never any system of apartheid or institutionalised discrimination against immigrants in Britain. Further, the immigrants came to Britain not only because of lack of opportunities in their native lands but also because they were needed in Britain. In the buoyant economic conditions of the 1950s and 1960s there was scarcity of labour, especially for heavy manual work. Just as the main influx of Irish labourers into Britain in the nineteenth and early twentieth centuries occurred during expansions of construction and heavy industry, so Commonwealth immigrants after World War Two graduated to jobs in the expanding car and engineering industries which were experiencing labour shortages. Immigrant labourers thus tended to complement, rather than compete with, the British work force; and they undertook work which indigenous workers were reluctant to do.

However, once the long economic upswing of the post-war generation turned into a decline, attitudes towards the immigrants began to change. In harsher times in the late 1960s and the 1970s they became a convenient scapegoat. This has been the response of a section of the population of any State, at any time, anywhere, when things start to go wrong: to pick on an easily identifiable minority and put the blame on them. The very features of the immigrants which made them so attractive to employers when labour was scarce, were seen by the British workers as posing a threat to their own position when the level of unemployment began to rise after 1968. The cheapness and mobility and apparent willingness of immigrant labour to work in poor conditions were perceived by British workers as undermining their own working conditions and employment.

The truth was that the immigrants did hard work for long hours at low wages primarily because they had to, not because they chose to. As a general rule, immigrant groups in any country are often trapped in a vicious circle from which it is difficult to escape. Usually poor and unskilled when they arrive in the country, they have either to migrate to new territory (as in the United States and Australasia), or, where there is none, they have to take any work and accommodation they can. As a result, they get a reputation among the indigenous population for accepting work at wages which may price local workers out of a job. The fact that immigrants can only get jobs at low wages means that they must also live in cheap housing. Yet the immigrants are often seen by the local population as being the cause of poor housing, rather than the victims of it. In the case of Commonwealth immigrants in Britain, there is little evidence that they lived in worse conditions than native Englishmen who earned the same low income. Nevertheless, once the idea was established that the immigrants were responsible for poor housing conditions, it tended to be self-perpetuating. Landlords would not lease their property to immigrants; and houses in good areas would not be sold to immigrants for fear of reducing property-values throughout the area. Consequently, the only accommodation immigrants could get was poor, and it was frequently leased at extortionate rents.

The methods by which the well-being of the immigrants could be improved were twofold. Firstly, self-help – the development of educational institutions and businesses by the immigrants themselves, without help from the native population. The Jewish immigrants in the nineteenth century, and the Asians in the post-World War Two period, were particularly successful in this. Yet, while their material standard of living improved, their success in developing self-contained economies within the areas of large cities where they settled did little to integrate them within British society. Self-sufficiency of immigrant communities only served to isolate them further from their adopted society.

The second method of helping the immigrants could directly assist their assimilation. It was Government action. The British Government took a lead against discrimination by introducing the Race Relations Act in 1968. This Act made discrimination in hiring and promoting workers on the basis of their race, religion, or creed illegal. It also made discrimination in letting or advertising housing illegal. In addition to these substantive measures, the Act established a Community Relations Commission responsible for education, public relations and social work to encourage harmonious race relations. Finally, the Act strengthened the powers of the Race Relations Board to conciliate in cases of discrimination.

The passage of this Act in the same year that Powellism became a significant political force in Britain accounts in large part for Britain's successful record in race relations during the 1970s, particularly when compared with the United States, or to the one area of the United Kingdom where ethnic tensions ran high, Northern Ireland. The Welfare State ensured that immigrant groups in Britain were not utterly deprived as were Negroes in the American ghettoes. The 1968 Race Relations Act further ensured that no connivance by the State was given to discrimination on the British mainland, as it was in Northern Ireland.

The Act was passed and enforced in spite of misgivings among a substantial minority of the British population, stirred up by Enoch Powell. This minority was not, with a few exceptions, positively racialist, as was shown by the abysmal performance of the racialist National Front Party in parliamentary elections during the 1970s, when they failed to save a single deposit in any constituency they contested. The outstanding feature of Powell's supporters was not overt racialism, but rather fear of the threat that immigrants posed to them in difficult economic conditions where there was intense competition for jobs, housing and other resources. This fear derived, not so much from racial hatred, as from the stereotype built up of the immigrant as someone who accepted worse living and working conditions than the native British were prepared to, and consequently who threatened to drag everyone down to his level.

One perfectly rational response, even if this stereotype was accurate, would have been to advocate greater efforts to improve the lot of the immigrants. This would have implied higher social spending, particularly to improve housing in the depressed inner city areas where the immigrants settled. This in turn would have required higher taxes to finance a construction programme. Such an idealistic response – to give up a share of their resources to help their fellow men, who were worse off than they were – was completely alien to Enoch Powell and his supporters. Their solution was one of reaction and repression; to stop the influx of immigrants and encourage those already in Britain to get out. The support for this response was never great enough to translate it into actual policy, but nevertheless it was not insignificant. Many commentators believed that Powellism was the crucial factor in the 1970 General Election result in Britain, when the Conservative Party wrested power from the Labour Party by a small majority. Dilip Hiro commented in his book, *Black British, White British,* "Of the sixty-six Conservative gains from Labour [in 1970] nearly two-thirds were in those constituencies which had a noticeable coloured population or were near to them, and/or had Powellite Tory candidates."

Ironically, the Conservative victory led to the appointment of Edward Heath as Prime Minister, the man who had sacked Powell from the Shadow Cabinet in 1968 after his first speech in Birmingham. Few had expected Heath to win the election; and the fact that he had, put him in an exceptionally strong position which enabled him to pass over the claims of Enoch Powell for office, even though Powell was the man whose influence may have been decisive in his election victory.

Nevertheless, greater emphasis was placed during the 1970s on restricting further immigration into Britain than on promoting the integration of those immigrants already in Britain, largely because of the impact of Powellism. Powell himself, however, remained an outsider within his own Party. Excluded from office, he developed during the period of the Heath Government into a one-man Opposition within the Conservative Party. He developed an entirely different approach from that of the Government, not only on the question of immigration, but also on Britain's relations with the European Common Market and the Government's role within the economy.

It was Powell's opposition to the Heath Government's decision to take Britain into the Common Market that led him to make the dramatic recommendation, in the course of the General Election campaign of February 1974, that his supporters should vote for the Labour Party. The basis on which he made this recommendation was that Labour in Government at least promised to give voters the chance to decide whether or not they wished to remain in the European Common Market in a referendum. Powell himself did not contest the election, on the grounds that it had been called on a bogus issue of whether the trade unions or the government governed Britain. But this was merely the pretext on which Powell left the House of Commons and effectively the Conservative Party. The truth was that he had been moving away from the mainstream of the Conservative Party steadily since 1968.

For the second time in four years Powell's role in the General Election may have been decisive. When the votes were counted, the Labour Party emerged as the largest single party in the House of Commons, though in a minority overall. The 1970 Tory lead of 43 seats over Labour was turned into a narrow victory for Labour in the February 1974 Election on account of the swing to Labour in two areas, the West Midlands and the North-West. Powell's opposition hit the Conservative Party hard in the West Midlands, where the swing to Labour radiated out through the West Midlands conurbation from the peak of Powellism in Wolverhampton, in which Powell's own Parliamentary seat had been. The following figures tell the story:

THE FEBRUARY 1974 GENERAL ELECTION

Area	*Swing to Labour*
Wolverhampton South-West	16·3%
Rest of Wolverhampton	12·7%
Constituencies adjacent to Wolverhampton	8·0%
Rest of the Black Country	6·1%
Birmingham	4·8%
Rest of the West Midlands conurbation	3·1%
Overall swing to Labour in the West Midlands conurbation	3·7%

Powell's intervention had helped Labour back into Government, to become the first minority Government Britain had experienced since 1931. Effective government was difficult in such a position, and another Election was called in October 1974, to resolve the situation. On this occasion the Labour Party gained a small absolute majority.

As for the maverick demagogue from Wolverhampton, he had burnt his boats with the Conservative Party for ever. His personal influence in British politics was on the wane. Those who actively supported him had never comprised more than a tiny proportion of the electorate, although in circumstances such as those of February 1974, when the result of the Election was literally on a knife-edge, their role was decisive. The reason why Powell failed to gain more support was that his analysis was wrong. The immigrants never posed the sort of threat that Powell argued they did, and legislation against discrimination helped to shape attitudes and ensure that they were never perceived as a threat by the vast majority of the British population.

Yet Enoch Powell's political career was not at an end. There was one part of the United Kingdom where the State's connivance with discrimination had set in train a tragic situation where political killings had become commonplace. In Northern Ireland, there was still a place for a politician whose appeal was based on his skill at playing on the fears of the voters. In October 1974, Enoch Powell was returned as Member of Parliament for the Ulster constituency of South Down.

On the British mainland, the defeat in the 1974 General Election led to a sharp swing to the right within the Conservative Party. If Powell himself was discredited, the influence of his ideas was nevertheless still strong. In 1975, Edward Heath was unceremoniously ejected from the leadership of the Conservative Party, to be replaced by Margaret Thatcher, whose whole outlook was closer to Powell's than to Heath's. Like Powell, Mrs Thatcher advocated strict control of the money supply as necessary for a prosperous economy; like Powell, but unlike Heath, she was less than an ardent European; and like Powell, but without his vitriolic demagoguery, she was unsympathetic to the aspirations of the coloured immigrants in Britain.

Her accession to the premiership in May 1979, following the Conservative victory at the General Election, heralded a new and harsher phase in race relations in Britain. Mrs Thatcher and her Government did not advocate racial discrimination or the repatriation of immigrants; but nevertheless certain events served to undermine the impartiality between different racial groups which the political leadership of the 1968–79 period had sought scrupulously to uphold.

Firstly, the Thatcher Government proposed to insert questions into the 1981 Census about the ethnic origins of the respondents. This proposal was dropped after a vigorous protest to it, when it became clear that many respondents would simply refuse to answer the question. Secondly, the Government introduced a Nationalities Bill in 1981, which proposed distinctive "classes" of British citizen, and would relegate recent immigrants to the status of second-class citizens in the eyes of the law. Thirdly, the recession which resulted from the Thatcher Government's economic policies caused a sharp increase in unemployment. This hit all groups in society, but it hit the coloured minorities hardest – unemployment among them increased twice as fast as among the general population during 1979–81. And fourthly, there were a number of incidents in which the Thatcher Government was not seen to be acting in a fair way, of which the most tragic was a fire at a party in Deptford, London, in January 1981, in which thirteen black youngsters died. No Government minister sent any expression of sympathy to the bereaved relatives; nor did the police appear to be investigating the case with the urgency or thoroughness which they would normally be expected to accord to such a tragedy. In the absence of any solution, rumours grew that the fire had been caused by a fire bomb attack carried out by supporters of a racialist group, such as the National Front. The whole affair did nothing to improve relations between the coloured community and the police, which were already poor in many areas because of the widespread belief that the "sus" law (whereby a citizen could be arrested if a police officer suspected him of intent to commit a crime, even if he had not actually done anything) was used as a pretext by the police to harass the blacks.

The grievances of the coloured communities inevitably increased. At their flash-points, these grievances exploded into violence such as those in the St Paul's district of Bristol in 1980, and in the Brixton district of London in 1981. On both occasions, attempted arrests of blacks by police officers sparked off major riots, in which many police and civilians were injured, and shops were looted.

A curious feature of the riots was that white youths joined the local blacks in throwing stones, bricks and other missiles against the police. This indicates that the riots were not true "race riots", but rather an expression of the animosity generally felt against the police, as agents of a government which was not seen to be applying the law impartially towards all its citizens, irrespective of their race. The riots were a clear warning-sign to the government of what might happen if it continued to turn a deaf ear to the coloured minorities and to connive in racial discrimination.

These warning signs should not have been necessary. The British Government already had a clear example of what the possible consequences were of State discrimination against a minority within it. This example lay on its own doorstep, in the tragedy of Northern Ireland.

The roots of the tragedy of Northern Ireland lie in the nature of its formation in 1921, as the result of a compromise cobbled together in an attempt to end Republican violence in Southern Ireland without provoking a backlash from the Protestants in the North. The compromise entailed the division of Ireland into two distinct political entities: the South became a self-governing dominion, while the six counties of the North with a Protestant majority remained in union with the rest of Britain. Northern Ireland was thus created to keep its Protestant majority happy, and the one-third of its population who were Catholics were never integrated into its structure of government.

Once this state of affairs was established, it became very difficult to break down. During the 1960s, a Civil Rights Association was formed to press for equality for Catholics within Northern Ireland, in elections, the provision of council housing, and employment opportunities. The Prime Minister of Northern Ireland of the time, Captain Terence O'Neill, was himself sympathetic to the aspirations of the civil rights campaign. But he was faced with opposition within his own Unionist Party, and first had to sack his Home Affairs minister, William Craig, and was subsequently faced with the resignation of the Commerce Minister, Brian Faulkner. O'Neill attempted to rally support for a policy of moderate reform by calling a General Election in Northern Ireland in February 1969; but he failed to attract any substantial Catholic vote to the Unionist Party, and was left with only a precarious majority. He resigned in April 1969.

His successors pursued a policy of repression, viewing the unrest among the Catholic community not as the expression of a legitimate desire for political reform, but as a strict question of law and order. In the summer of 1969, the British Army was sent into Northern Ireland following clashes between Catholics and Protestants in Londonderry and Belfast. The Army was initially welcomed by the Catholics as a neutral peace-keeping force, but as it became increasingly clear that the British Government at Westminster proposed no substantive reforms, and that the Army would act merely as an arm of the Protestant State, relations between the Army and the Catholic community worsened. In response to the escalation in violence, the policy of repression was hardened. In August 1971, internment – the imprisonment without trial of suspected terrorists – was introduced, and was applied only to Catholics. This caused a further heightening of tensions, and was exploited by the Provisional Irish Republican Army (I.R.A.), which styled itself as an army of liberation and began to move into Catholic districts in urban centres. The violence reached a peak in the months following internment; until finally, in March 1972, the British Government prorogued the Northern Ireland Parliament and introduced direct rule of the province from Westminster.

The British Government then moved to restore the rule of law in Northern Ireland. Troop reinforcements were brought in, and in July 1972 the I.R.A. was cleared from the Catholic ghettoes during

Operation Motorman. The Government next attempted to introduce political reforms, by holding elections for a Northern Ireland Assembly on the basis of proportional representation, which were followed by the establishment of a power-sharing executive for the province which included both Protestant and Catholic ministers. But the Executive lasted only five months before it was brought down by a strike of the Protestant loyalist Ulster Workers' Council in May 1974.

Despite later efforts by successive British governments to introduce political reforms, there was never any real possibility that direct rule could be phased out again during the 1970s. With little prospect of a political solution, the violence continued during the 1970s and early 1980s, although on a lesser scale than during 1971/72. By the end of 1982, more than 2,200 people had died in the troubles. Over the same period, the economic fabric of Northern Ireland gradually crumbled in the absence of new investment, which was bound to be insufficient until the physical security of investors and their factories was ensured.

The tragedy of Northern Ireland provides a terrible warning of the possible consequences of State discrimination against a minority within it. Once a minority has been excluded from equal participation in the political process, it may be forced to set up its own institutions for education, social welfare, and production; and these institutions then serve to reinforce the barriers between the minority and the rest of society. In the case of the British mainland, the racial minorities were not driven into underprivileged enclaves, but were given equal access to State education, public housing, and the social services. But in Northern Ireland, a combination of an educational system divided on religious lines, and discrimination in the provision of council housing and jobs, served to cut off the Catholics from the Protestant majority.

Perhaps in the final analysis there is no chance of resolving the problems of Northern Ireland until the communities themselves are destroyed; until the sectarian educational system in Northern Ireland is dismantled, and vigorous action is taken to reconstruct the economy of the Province, so that Protestants and Catholics are forced to learn and work together for their common good. Yet the chances of achieving such an initiative from Westminster seemed increasingly remote as the 1980s rolled on. The reason was not merely lack of political will on the part of the British Government; it was also that the commitment of required resources became increasingly difficult as the Government grappled unsuccessfully to arrest the decline of the British economy.

II

The first principle upon which any social organisation operates is to protect the interests of its own members first. Only when the position of its own members is secure can the organisation afford to make concessions to other groups. The same principle applies with political parties. Only when they have secured the interests of their own supporters can they reach beyond and make concessions to other groups.

Up to the late 1960s, sustained economic growth meant that the position of the groups which formed the basis of power for each of Britain's major political parties was improving year by year. So each political party when in office could keep its own supporters happy, and there was enough left from the growing national cake for bigger slices for other people too. But once the national cake stopped growing, more of the cake for one group of people necessarily meant less for others. In consequence, competition for resources between different groups in society intensified.

The intensification of conflict was most evident in Northern Ireland, which had been the poorest region of the United Kingdom even in the years of growing affluence in the 1950s and 1960s. In Northern Ireland, the conflict took the form of a recrudescence of a primitive form of tribalism. Each of the two main tribes, Catholics and Protestants, tried to protect their own and reacted to threats to their interests with growing intransigence. Any political leader suspected of softening in his attitude to the rival tribe was quickly discarded.

The conflict could have taken the same form on mainland Britain, with the white indigenous population turning on the coloured immigrants. That it did not, may be attributed in large part to strong leadership by the Government which helped to shape the attitudes of the population and confirm the feeling that racialism was abhorrent. This may be regarded as one of the real achievements of the liberal consensus in Britain.

Strong action by Government as a neutral arbiter between competing groups was not, however, possible in industry. The reason was: both of the two major political parties had their roots deep in industry; the Labour Party relied on the trade unions for the bulk of its funds, while the Conservative Party relied on business for its finance. So neither Party when in office could be seen as independent of the conflict in industry which it sought to resolve.

Thus, if either party acted in a way that favoured the interests of their own supporters in industry, the other side could accuse them of acting in a manner determined by party political considerations. Ironically, each party could only claim to be acting "in the national interest" with any degree of credibility if it pursued policies which were actually inimical to its own natural supporters. So it was that the Conservative Government of Edward Heath imposed price and dividend restraint on companies towards the end of its term of office – actions which contributed to the drastic slump in corporate profits of 1973–75. Then the Labour Government which succeeded it introduced the only incomes policy ever to reduce the real wages of trade unionists.

But as the recession worsened, the patience of each party's supporters with policies which hurt them became increasingly strained. Consequently, a new generation of politicians emerged to displace the consensus politicians who had tried to act according to the national interest, even when it hurt their own supporters. The new generation – led by Margaret Thatcher in the Conservative Party, and Tony Benn in the Labour Party – were equipped with ideologies which unequivocally favoured their own supporters at the expense of the other side. In the Labour Party the "moderates" of the centre lost ground to the new Left Wing, which advocated the extension of public ownership and the imposition of further controls on the British economy to ensure full employment of the work-force. In the Conservative Party, the liberal wing was displaced after the 1974 General Elections by the monetarist Right.

The economic policies of the Conservative Government elected in May, 1979, marked a clear break with the past. The Callaghan Government had been pursuing monetary control through wage restraint since 1976; but this watered-down form of monetarism had been implemented with less than unanimous consent among the Government's own ranks. In particular, restraint of Government expenditure was accepted as a necessary evil to be suffered until the economic situation improved, rather than as a permanent feature.

By contrast, the Government of Margaret Thatcher which succeeded it regarded the cutback of Government expenditure as positively desirable. After the fall of Edward Heath, the Conservative Party had adopted the economic philosophy of monetarism whose high priest was the Nobel Prizewinner in Economics, Professor Milton Friedman. Since its conversion in the mid-1970s, the Conservative Party had preached the new gospel of monetarism with all the unquestioning faith and enthusiasm of St Paul after his vision on the road to Damascus.

Monetarism offered to the new Government the means to achieve its two central objectives. The first of these objectives was the reduction of the rate of inflation; the second was the rolling back of the public sector and the encouragement of private enterprise. The monetarist approach to economic policy-making entailed control of the money supply as the means by which the rate of inflation would be brought down, and restraint of Government expenditure as the means by which the money supply would be controlled and resources encouraged to move from the public sector into the private sector of the economy. It is important to distinguish between these two elements in monetarist economics, for they are by no means equivalent. In particular, acceptance of the view that the increase in the money supply has been the most important cause of inflation in Britain since the Second World War, and that restraint of monetary growth is the best method of reducing the rate of inflation, does not imply acceptance of the view that expansion of Government spending was the main cause of the increase in the money supply and that therefore cutbacks in Government spending were required to control the money supply. Each of the two propositions must be appraised independently, and their accuracy evaluated on their own merits independently of the other.

The British monetarist orthodoxy related the two, and argued that the application of Keynesian demand management techniques had not only generated a monetary inflation, but had also reduced the rate of growth of productive capacity in the British economy. Thus, Bacon and Eltis in their book *Britain's Economic Problem: Too Few Producers* argued that, in recession, it had been cheaper and easier for Government to absorb some of the unemployed labour force by expanding the (public sector) social services, where no plant and machinery was required; rather than by expanding industry, where any permanent employment had associated capital costs. But the consequence of this policy was that, when the economy expanded again after the recession, the labour employed by the social services and in Government administration was unavailable for employment by industry, and full employment in the economy was attained at a lower level of industrial production than would have been achieved had the Government never intervened at all during the recession.

The new orthodoxy further argued that increases in public expenditure had reduced the volume of funds available to the private sector for investment. Government spending is funded by taxation, and additionally, if spending exceeds taxation revenue, by borrowing. If extra Government spending is funded by taxation revenue, then this in itself is non-inflationary: it merely diverts resources from the private to the public sector of the economy. If extra Government spending is funded by borrowing, on the other hand, it is only non-inflationary to the extent that this borrowing draws on real savings of the non-bank private sector. If private sector savings are inadequate to finance Government borrowing, then the effect of the borrowing is to inflate the money supply. Monetary inflation results in a price inflation, which reduces the real value of private incomes – so that the inflation may be regarded as a form of tax levied by the Government on the private sector, and one of the means by which real resources are transferred from the private sector to the Government.

The monetarists argued that the acceleration in inflation after 1967 could be attributed to an expansion in money supply, and that one of the main factors in this expansion was an increase in Government spending. They further argued that the financing of this spending had been borne largely by private sector profits rather than by wages and salaries. The reason for this was that resistance to reductions in their real wages among workers generated increased trade union pressure for higher money wages to offset the higher levels of taxation and retail prices. In the words of Nigel Denton, writing in the *Accountant* magazine of June 26th, 1980:

The Treasury coffers have been filled . . . at the expense of a

> combined fall in the share [of national income] of labour and capital. The resistance of labour, management as well as employees, to the erosion of take-home pay, via taxation, has meant that taxes have been pushed onto profits. If accountants had been measuring company performance by value added over the past 25 years, and clearly isolating the different claims on it, labour and capital would not have appeared to be so much in conflict, but rather united against their common assailant – taxation.

The New Orthodoxy went on to argue that reduction of profitability caused by Government spending had adverse effects on investment. Retained profits are the cheapest and most easily obtainable source of investment finance for companies. A reduction in profits therefore forces companies either to cut back their investment plans, or to borrow money from outside the company to fund investment. But borrowing from outside at fixed interest rates carries greater risks than financing from retained earnings, because loans must be repaid and the interest payments due on them must be met, whereas there are no contractual requirements regarding the servicing of retained earnings. Consequently, if a company's dependence on externally-raised loans increases, so too does its vulnerability to bankruptcy in time of economic recession. If its earnings fall below the level projected, a company can postpone or cancel dividend payments to its own shareholders, but it cannot indefinitely postpone loan repayments and interest payments. Ultimately, its creditors will foreclose and the company will be declared bankrupt. So, according to the New Orthodoxy, the reduction in corporate profitability which occurred in Britain during the 1970s explained both the fall in the rate of gross investment, and the sharp increase in the number of company liquidations. And the cause of these trends, the New Orthodoxy argued, was excessive Government spending.

The New Orthodoxy postulated that higher Government spending had crowded the private sector out of access to the means of production: labour and investment finance: and had diverted these resources from sectors in which they would have contributed to the final output of saleable goods and services, to sectors where they did not. In so doing, Government spending had eroded the productive capacity of the British economy and reduced the level of employment it could support. So far from Keynesian demand-management techniques sustaining full employment of the labour force, they had undermined it.

The solution advocated by the New Orthodoxy was the rolling back of the Government sector, by cutting administrative overheads, and letting the private sector undertake certain operations previously in Government hands and, where Government still ran operations, to subject them to the disciplines of the market by cutting subsidies. In this way, the Public Sector Borrowing Requirement – the amount of money the Government needed to borrow in order to finance its expenditure – would be brought under control, and so would the money supply and the rate of inflation. In the short term, these measures might cause a rise in unemployment if increases in earnings exceeded increases in productivity; but in the longer term inflation would be reduced and resources released for the private sector to build up the productive capacity of the economy.

In its favour, one can agree that the economic analysis developed by the New Orthodoxy at least offered a coherent explanation of the problems which afflicted the British economy in the 1970s: the problems of inflation, combined with secularly rising unemployment and company liquidations, and falling real investment and the consequent erosion of productive capacity. The question is whether the monetarist story tells the true tale of the crumbling of consensus after 1968.

As far as its explanation of inflation as predominantly a *monetary* phenomenon is concerned, the proposition that inflation in Britain since 1945 has been *principally* caused by the excessive growth of the money supply looks suspect in the light of international experience. The statistics reveal that growth of the money supply has been lower in Britain than in the non-communist world taken as a whole since 1952, and yet the rate of inflation has been higher in Britain than in the rest of the world. The secular pattern can be seen by looking at the five-year averages (for source, see Statistical Appendix II).

The reason why lower rates of monetary growth have been associated with higher rates of inflation in the U.K. than in the non-communist world as a whole is fairly clear. Inflation exists when the growth of monetary demand exceeds the growth of physical output to satisfy that demand, and consequently pulls up the

	per annum averages			
	World		*U.K.*	
Period	*Rate of inflation*	*Rate of growth of money supply*	*Rate of inflation*	*Rate of growth of money supply*
1952–54	2·2	5·4	4·7	2·9
1955–59	3·1	5·5	3·3	1·9
1960–64	3·6	7·5	2·8	3·7
1965–69	4·8	8·2	4·2	6·0
1970–74	8·5	11·7	12·2	17·2
1975–79	11·5	11·0	15·6	10·6

general price level. The true culprit for inflation in Britain has not been either excessive growth of monetary demand, as the monetarists argue, or excessive increases in nominal wages, as the liberal institutionalists argue. Both of these have in fact been low by international standards. *The prime cause of inflation in Britain has been the sluggish growth of the productive capacity of the British economy*. The rate of growth of industrial production in the non-communist world (according to the data presented in the I.M.F. Survey of November 12th, 1979) averaged nearly 6 per cent per annum in the 1954–79 period. The rate of growth of industrial production in Britain over the same period averaged less than 2·75 per cent each year. This implied that any given increase in the money supply or in money wages was not met from increases in real output in Britain to the same extent as in the world as a whole; instead, the prices of existing output were pulled up.

So the first fallacy of the monetarist orthodoxy has been that it has addressed itself to the less important side of the demand-supply equation, by attempting to hold back inflation by restraining the growth of monetary demand, rather than by increasing the capacity of the economy to meet that demand.

The second main tenet of the monetarists is that Government spending has been the main cause of the expansion of the money supply. The growth of sterling M3 is equal to domestic credit expansion plus any increase in foreign exchange and net non-deposit liabilities. Domestic credit is in turn composed of two major components: bank lending to the overseas and private sectors (which is the private sector's contribution to domestic credit expansion), and the borrowing requirement of the public sector, less that part of it absorbed by the non-bank private sector (which is the public sector's contribution). The breakdown of the components of domestic credit expansion given in the Statistical Appendices show no close correlation between the Public Sector Borrowing Requirement, either in gross terms or net of sales of public sector debt to the non-bank private sector, and the growth of money supply. In particular, in the key years of 1969 to 1973 when the explosive growth of domestic credit occurred, the main impulse in monetary growth came from private bank lending and not from the Public Sector Borrowing Requirement. The evidence of the past decade or so is that the Public Sector Borrowing Requirement has been greatest in years of economic recession, when the rate of growth of national income and industrial output has been lowest. Thus, the Public Sector Borrowing Requirement (P.S.B.R.) reached successive peaks in 1967, 1975 and 1979: each years of recession in the real economy. The P.S.B.R. was high in these years as a direct result of the recessions because as the real economy goes into down-turn, so the level of employment and spending falls – and consequently so too does real Government revenue, which is raised mainly from taxes on income and spending. At the same time, the level of Government spending on unemployment benefits rises during recession. Thus, the gap between Government revenue and expenditure which has to be funded by borrowing tends to vary inversely with the rate of economic growth; and the increase in the Public Sector Borrowing Requirement which has occurred since the late 1960s may be regarded as a natural consequence of the decline which has occurred in the rate of economic growth since then, rather than as an independent cause of monetary growth and, through it, of the rate of inflation.

The major factor in the explosion in the money supply in the early 1970s was private sector bank lending, and there were two main factors underlying it. The first was the rapid growth in the world supply of money, which was related to large deficits in the Balance of Payments of the United States. Much of this money found its way into London, as one of the traditional centres of international finance, which gave British banks a larger monetary base on which to build their lending.

The second factor was the reform in the way in which the banks were regulated by the Government, brought about by the White Paper on "Competition and Credit Control" of 1971. This permitted clearing banks to build a larger pyramid of lending on any given monetary base. Ironically, the adoption of methods of bank regulation advocated by monetarists – which were intended to control the supply of money through the operation of price mechanism – became instead one of the most important causes of the explosive growth of both money supply and inflation during the early 1970s.

To understand why, it is necessary to retrace the story of monetary management in the U.K. since 1945.

III

The Keynesian approach to monetary control, which operated between the Second World War and 1971, was to keep interest rates low (so that productive investment would not be discouraged) and restrict the availability of credit by direct controls on consumer borrowing, and by means of "Open Market Operations" by the Bank of England.

The purpose of Open Market Operations was the control of the monetary base of commercial banks on which the banks built their lending. These operations entailed trading in long-dated Government stocks (or gilts as they are more popularly known), and in Treasury Bills of three months' maturity issued by the British Treasury at a discount on their face value of £100. Treasury Bills offered banks and other institutions trading on the money market an opportunity to earn a return on their liquid funds.

Treasury Bills became the most important short-term asset traded on the money market during the Second World War, when they were used as a means of mopping up idle funds in banks. The Government issued Treasury Bills at rates similar to those of first-class commercial bills, and they were purchased by Discount Houses which borrowed the money they needed to buy the bills from the commercial banks. Essentially, Treasury Bills were a Keynesian tool designed to achieve an *ex ante* equality between savings (by private individuals and institutions) and investment and war-related spending (by the Government), in order to ensure full employment of resources in wartime; and to shift resources from the private sector into war production.

The technique was continued after the war. When it appeared

that monetary demand was running ahead of productive capacity and causing retail price inflation, the Government would issue more Treasury Bills, in return for which it would receive cheques payable by the commercial banks. Once these cheques were submitted to the banks, their reserves contracted and the banks would be forced to restrict their advances to the private sector.

In practice, the application of cash squeezes through sales of Treasury Bills was restricted by the Government's reliance on Discount Houses to provide a safe market for short-term Government debt. This meant that the Discount Houses could not reduce their holdings of Treasury Bills significantly in times of a cash squeeze. If commercial banks recalled part of the loans the Discount Houses had originally raised to buy Treasury Bills, the Discount Houses would be forced to borrow from non-bank institutions: thereby bidding up the general level of interest rates. Thus, monetary policy would be successful only if the Government was prepared to see interest rates rise. But the policy of successive Governments during the 1950s and 1960s was to maintain low interest rates, in order to encourage borrowing for investment purposes and to minimise the burden of interest payments on its own debt.

Sales of Treasury Bills were also restricted by the fear that equilibrium in the money market was unstable. The notion was that if the Government sought to curtail the money supply by the sale of Treasury Bills, it would squeeze the liquid reserves of the commercial banks and Discount Houses. The banks and Discount Houses would then be forced to sell securities in order to maintain a safe liquidity ratio. But expectations of non-bank financial institutions and private traders of a fall in the general price-level of securities might cause them to hold back from buying the extra securities, and security prices would fall further. So instead of the demand for securities expanding in response to a fall in their prices, it would contract. In order to avoid the downward spiral in the price of securities, and hence an upward spiral in interest rates, the Bank of England would step in to buy securities and keep interest rates low. Thus, in periods of supposed monetary restraint during the 1950s and 1960s, the Bank of England often became a net buyer of securities, including Government stock, and consequently the commercial banks were under little pressure to contract their lending.

Until the late 1960s, there was little concern about this, as there was widespread acceptance of the orthodox Keynesian proposition that the amount of money in an economy was not a particularly significant factor in determining the overall level of economic activity and prices. But during the later 1960s and 1970s, the ideas of the new monetarist orthodoxy gained support, and the importance of restricting monetary growth was increasingly accepted. Rather than do this by allowing a general rise in interest rates – which would cost the Government money in higher payments on the National Debt – Governments of the 1960s attempted to control the money supply directly, leaving interest rates unaffected. Hence a structure of direct controls on commercial banks was gradually introduced: ranging from directions from the Bank of England to commercial banks as to the amount and type of lending they should undertake (introduced in 1964); to compulsory Special Deposits by the commercial banks in the Bank of England, which could be withdrawn only when the Bank of England gave permission, which cut directly at the banks' base of liquid assets (introduced in 1965).

This structure of direct controls came under attack for the alleged misallocations of credit and inhibition of competition between the commercial banks in which it resulted. The Heath Government which came to office in 1970 stated its intention of reverting to the price mechanism as the means of allocating credit. Its proposals for reform of the money markets were embodied in its White Paper on "Competition and Credit Control", published in 1971.

The purpose of the new monetary policy was the tighter control of the supply of money in the economy, even if this implied high interest rates. This reflected the greater importance that was being attributed to the money supply by academic economists. As Milton Friedman had written in 1968, "Monetary policy can prevent money itself from being a major source of economic disturbance . . . [and] can contribute to offsetting major disturbances in the economic system arising from other sources." (*American Economic Review*.) Friedman's own recommendation was that the rate of increase in the money supply should be equal to the underlying growth of the economy's productive capacity through time; because he argued that a faster rate would give rise to inflation, and a slower rate to unemployment of productive resources greater than that level justified by the need to maintain price stability – the so-called "natural" rate of unemployment. Friedman observed that, "Periods of relative stability of monetary growth have also been periods of relative stability in economic activity, both in the U.S.A. and other countries." ("The Role of Monetary Policy", *American Economic Review*, 1968.)

Friedman postulated that attempts to peg interest rates (such as had been made in the U.K. in the 1950s and 1960s) were inimical to stable monetary policy. To keep interest rates low, the Central Bank (the Bank of England in the U.K.) would have to buy securities to avoid a squeeze on the cash base of the commercial banking sector. "In the process," wrote Friedman, "[the Central Bank] increases the quantity of reserves available to banks, hence the amount of bank credit, and ultimately the total quantity of money." (*American Economic Review*, 1968.) A greater quantity of money would eventually result in a higher level of monetary expenditure, which would raise prices and reduce the real value of any given amount of money. "Let the higher rate of monetary growth produce rising prices, and let the public come to expect that prices will continue to rise. Borrowers will then be willing to pay, and lenders will then demand, higher interest rates." So in order to keep interest rates low, the Central Bank would have to make successively larger open market purchases of Treasury Bills and other securities. But it could only do this for so long; in the end, retail price inflation in the goods markets would force it to let interest rates rise, or inflation would accelerate to astronomic levels, and the whole fabric of the economy would be endangered. Hence the "Friedman Paradox", that "historically, high and rising nominal interest-rates have been associated with rapid growth in the quantity of money . . . [while] low and falling interest-rates have been associated with slow growth of the quantity of money." (Friedman, *American Economic Review*, 1968.)

The power of the argument of Friedman and the monetarists rested not in a mere preference for the control of the supply of money rather than its cost (the rate of interest), but in the view that interest rates could not be regulated for any length of time, and if the monetary authorities attempted to impose such regulation they could do so only by allowing an explosive growth of the money supply and subsequently the rate of inflation.

The "Competition and Credit Control" White Paper marked the first major shift towards the Friedman school of thought in Britain. The purpose of "Competition and Credit Control" was to end Government regulation of the money markets, and leave the forces of supply and demand to determine interest rates. The Bank of England withdrew its automatic support from the gilt-edged market, and only guaranteed to buy gilt-edged stock with less than one year to maturity. The price at which short-term Government stock would be traded was also released from Government control: the agreed interest rate for a Treasury Bill issue was ended, and Discount Houses were only committed to buy Treasury Bills at interest rates to be negotiated, which would rise with successive tranches of Treasury Bills on offer. "Competition and Credit Control" also proposed measures to introduce free competition into the private sector, just as it did into the public sector of the money markets. The commercial banks were instructed to abandon their interest rate cartel, so that the interest rates they offered would be genuinely competitive. All commercial banks were required to have a minimum ratio of liquid assets/total assets of 12½ per cent, and reserve asset ratios were also laid down for the first time for non-bank financial institutions. The application of reserve ratio requirements to all finance houses, and not just commercial banks, was intended to reduce the opportunities for clearing banks to increase their share of a reduced total of liquid reserve assets by attracting them away from non-bank institutions.

Some direct controls, notably Special Deposits, remained in force. However, the fact that they were to be applied uniformly through the money market would, it was hoped, avoid any distortion of the forces of supply and demand, and enable the market to work more efficiently.

Paradoxically, the adoption of a monetarist approach to the management of the money market led to an unprecedented explosion in bank-created credit. Monetary growth (as measured by the increase in sterling M3), which had never exceeded 10 per cent in any previous year in the post-war era, rose 14 per cent in 1971, 24 per cent in 1972, and 26 per cent in 1973. The new reserve requirements, which stipulated that banks should hold 12½ per cent of their assets in liquid form, in fact proved far laxer than the cash base requirements they superseded. The commercial banks were able to reduce their ratio of liquid to total assets; or, to put the same thing slightly differently, they were able to build a much greater pyramid of lending on a given monetary base. At the same time, the size of their monetary base was growing because of the international monetary explosion of the late 1960s and early 1970s.

So the experience of Britain, far from supporting the so-called "Friedman Paradox", in fact supported the exact opposite. The neo-Keynesian orthodoxy which held sway until the late 1960s succeeded in maintaining relatively low interest rates while incidentally keeping monetary growth within reasonable bounds. There was no evidence of the explosive monetary growth which Friedman hypothesised in consequence of a cheap money policy. Conversely, when Friedmanite monetary methods were adopted, the consequence was an explosive rise both in money supply and in the general level of interest rates. The rise in interest rates did not succeed in choking off demand for credit from the private sector, because much of the growth in demand was fuelled by a speculative boom in the property market. As long as property speculators believed that property prices would increase at a rate higher than the rate of interest, they were prepared to borrow to finance property purchases. And as long as speculative demand for property accelerated, the prices of property rose in the way the speculators anticipated, so that their speculations were self-fulfilling – in the classic manner of speculative booms ever since the South Sea Bubble.

But, also in the classic manner of speculative booms, the property boom of 1971–73 came to a sudden and dramatic end, when the growth of speculative demand began to slow. This occurred when some of the more farsighted speculators decided to get out while they were ahead. With property prices easing, the remaining speculators who had borrowed heavily to finance their property investments found they were unable to sell at a profit to repay their loans, and they went into default. With their debtors in default, many of the banks which had lent to the speculators found themselves dangerously short of liquid funds with which to meet payments to their depositors. In late 1973, a run began on the London & County Bank, and this was followed by a general run on secondary banks by creditors worried that their deposits would not be honoured.

To prevent a disastrous panic, the Bank of England and the major clearing banks launched a rescue operation, and lent to the secondary banks to enable them to meet the withdrawl of deposits. The Bank of England and the major clearing banks put up £1·2 billion for the secondary banks, and the Bank of England extended a further £600m. in the rescue operation independently of the clearing banks. Even so, eight of the twenty-six companies "rescued" went out of business, and the banks which undertook the rescue operation had to write off around £200m. in bad debts. In addition, reported the *Economist* of May 6th, 1978, "The Bank of England has proably laid out at least another £50m. for the rescue operations it mounted on its own, £30m. for Slater Walker Securities and £18m. for Edward Bates. Some four years later, the lifeboat operation still has more than £650m. tied up in supports." Most of this money was effectively provided by the British taxpayer through the Bank of England, and represented a waste of resources that could have been better used in the provision of education or health services, or investment in infra-structure.

"Competition and Credit Control" was not the only factor in the property boom of the early 1970s. Nevertheless, without the reforms introduced by that White Paper, it is hardly conceivable that the credit explosion which financed property speculation would have occurred.

The lesson was clear. A rise in interest rates alone might not be sufficient to control the growth of bank-created credit and hence the money supply. This lesson was not lost on the British Government. Targets were established for the growth of sterling M3, the most commonly used definition of money supply. To ensure that the growth of sterling M3 did not regain the levels of 26 per cent per annum attained in 1972 and 1973, some degree of direct control was introduced over it.

The main instrument of direct control used by the Government, through the Bank of England, over the growth of bank-created credit after 1973 was the supplementary deposit scheme, or "corset". The corset was intended to curb bank lending by setting a limit on the rate of growth of the commercial banks' interest-bearing liabilities.

The corset did not achieve its intended effect, however. Government's intervention in the money market after 1973, like its intervention in the labour market in the period 1966–79, merely distorted the way in which the forces of supply and demand made themselves felt, and led to the creation of new markets specifically designed to evade Government regulations. In the labour market, this evasion had been through the growth of the "two-tier" bargaining structure. In the money market, it was through the development of forms of near-money which did not fall within the definition of sterling M3.

Thus, holdings of bank-accepted commercial bills ("acceptances") increased rapidly. These were bills issued by private companies which commercial banks promised to honour if they were presented; and they had the useful dual function of being a marketable asset for the companies which issued them – and so provided a means by which they could raise cash – yet not constituting an interest-bearing liability for the commercial banks. Because they were not an interest-bearing liability, they did not fall within the corset. Thus, when in July 1979 two of the Big Four British commercial banks exceeded the corset limits and were penalised by having to deposit 5 per cent of the excess interest-free with the Bank of England, they responded in the following month by increasing their acceptances by 19 per cent. This exemplifies the general principle: that the corset did not effectively restrain the growth of bank-created credit; but merely altered the form which this growth took. The experience of the corset proved "Goodhart's Law", which states that any monetary series which the authorities attempt to control instantly becomes meaningless, because both the commercial banks and the companies and individuals to whom they lend will connive in their common interest to develop new forms of money which fall outside the monetary series in which the authorities are interested.

Some conclusions can be drawn from the experience of thirty-five years of monetary management since the Second World War.

It used to be thought that monetary policy could either fix the *price* of money – that is, the interest rate; or the *amount* of money in the economic system – the money supply; but not both simultaneously.

Until the 1970s, the primary objective of monetary policy was to keep the price of money low, and to allow money supply to grow accordingly. This was largely a consequence of the overall adoption of Keynesian methods of economic management. But it was also in part making a virtue of necessity, since there was no consensus as to *how* the Bank of England should control the creation of credit by the commercial banks. The experience of the 1970s indicated that in practice limitations might be set to sales of Treasury Bills by the willingness of the private sector non-bank institutions to buy them. If pension and insurance funds were already replete with Treasury Bills and long-term Government stock, they might be reluctant to unbalance their portfolios by buying more Government stock, no matter how high the interest rate offered. Even if the institutions were prepared to increase their holdings of Government stocks, an increase in the interest rates on those stocks might perversely cause them to refrain from buying the stocks in the expectation that their yields would rise still further as the Government became desperate to sell them.

The Bank of England's abdication of control over the money supply in preference for low interest rates gave Britain a quarter-century of monetary stability between 1945 and 1970. The destabilisation of the monetary system after 1970 occurred as a consequence of international disturbances outside the UK's control. It did not arise because of an inevitable tendency of the money supply to accelerate if the authorities sought to hold the interest rate below some "natural" equilibrium level.

Conversely, the replacement of a cheap money policy in 1971 by a monetary policy intended to restrict the money supply, ushered in a decade of unprecedented acceleration both in the money supply – however defined – and in the general level of interest rates in the U.K. The experience of a decade of this form of monetary management must give rise to the conclusion that it was a failure.

The conventional explanation of this failure is that of the opponents of monetarist theory – who argue that the failure arose because the basic monetarist assumption of a causal relationship between the growth of the money supply and the rate of inflation after a lag is false. But this explanation cannot hold water. Certainly, as the Conservative politician John Biffen admitted in early 1980, "There is no mechanistic and succinctly demonstrable link between the money supply and a subsequent change in inflation." Nevertheless, while the link between money supply and inflation may not be mechanistic, the evidence is that it does exist when productive capacity is fully employed. The comparative weakness of the measured relationship between money supply and inflation in the case of the United Kingdom probably tells more about the flaws of Sterling M3 as a measure of money supply in a regulated money market than about the true relationship between money and prices.

The real reason why the New Orthodoxy failed in its management of the money markets is because it did not understand the nature of the relationship between the money markets and the rest of the economy. Whereas monetary management during the Keynesian era had been a *means* to achieving the ends of the real economy – to mobilising resources to war, and then in the post-war era to sustaining full employment of resources – since the advent of monetarism the attainment of monetary control has become an end in itself. Instead of monetary policies being adapted to the needs of the real economy, the monetarists believed that the real economy would respond to a tight monetary policy, for example by inducing lower wage demands in the labour market. The monetarists were correct in arguing that extraneous monetary disturbances can disrupt the real economy, by causing inflation and generating general uncertainty about the future trend in monetary values.

But the converse also holds. That is, monetary stability is not possible unless the real economy is in balance. This was the lesson of the attempt to go back to the Gold Standard in 1925–31, and it is also the lesson of the present-day failure of monetarism. Monetary control alone is not sufficient to achieve equilibrium in the real economy; and if monetary policies are applied with no regard to the workings of the real economy, they may actually worsen its problems.

IV

The first part of the economic strategy advocated by the New Orthodoxy entailed the reduction of the rate of inflation by the control of the quantity of money in the economy. In the private sector, this control was to be achieved by allowing the price of money, the rate of interest, to rise to whatever level was necessary to choke off the growth of bank-created credit; but this technique failed and the experience of the 1970s indicated that the private sector's demand for bank-created credit was not particularly responsive to changes in the rate of interest.

In the public sector, the New Orthodoxy advocated cutbacks in public expenditure to reduce the Public Sector Borrowing Requirement. However, retrenchment of public expenditure did not prove easy to implement during the 1970s, when growth in the private sector was less buoyant than it had been during the 1950s or 1960s. The downturn in economic growth simultaneously increased the demands made on public expenditure, particularly for unemployment and related benefits, while tending to erode the productive base from which government revenue was raised. So it was difficult to keep public sector recurrent expenditure under control; and in practice the monetarist governments of the 1970s found it easier to wield the axe on capital spending.

In constant (1975) prices, public sector investment (excluding dwellings) was cut from around £7 billion p.a. in 1973–75 to only £5 billion by 1979. Private sector investment measured on the same basis grew from £9½ billion to £11 billion over the same period; but this growth was not sufficient to offset the cuts in the public sector investment programme. This slump in investment meant that insufficient job opportunities were generated to absorb new entrants into the labour market, and inevitably the level of unemployment rose. Even worse in the long run, it undermined the productive capacity of the British economy, as shown by the fall in the index of manufacturing production after 1973. It therefore undermined the country's ability to ever regain the conditions of full employment with steadily rising standards which had been achieved in 1945–68.

While they carried out drastic cuts of capital expenditure, the monetarist Government of the post-1971 period failed to exercise effective control over the recurrent expenditure of the public sector, and particularly the public sector pay bill. The cyclical fluctuations in the Public Sector Borrowing Requirement (P.S.B.R.) over its rising secular trend can be largely explained by the control (or lack of it) exercised over public sector pay during the 1970s. Thus, the pay explosion of 1973–75 is reflected in a sharp increase in P.S.B.R. in those years; the temporarily successful incomes policy of the mid-1970s succeeded in reining back the P.S.B.R. during 1975–77; and the collapse of that policy after the winter of 1978–79 led to an upsurge in the P.S.B.R. thereafter.

The Thatcher Government which came to office in 1979 was committed to holding back the current expenditure of the public sector. The stated target of Mrs Thatcher herself was to reduce the number of employees of central Government by some 100,000 or 15 per cent during her five-year term of office between 1979 and 1984. It is too early to judge whether these targets will be met; but it is probably not premature to state that if they are achieved, it will not be through genuine improvements in efficiency – because there is no strategy to make such improvements. The manpower targets will be met, if at all, not by improving the efficiency with which the public services are provided, but by reducing the quality and quantity of those services.

The Thatcher Government's own published public expenditure plans were clear in their implications. The real volume of spending on defence, law and order, and payments to the unemployed (whose numbers were expected to rise) was projected to increase. Cuts were to be implemented in aid, the social services, and the Government's capital expenditure programme. But these were so close to their feasible minimum by 1979 that substantial savings from them were not possible.

The "deus ex machina" by which the public sector's financial position was to be transformed during the lifetime of the Thatcher Government were the nationalised industries, which were assumed to recover from a deficit of £2·3 billion in 1979–80 to a surplus of £0·4 billion (in 1979 prices) by 1983–84. These projections were based on the elimination of losses in coal, steel, and shipbuilding, and an increase in the real level of energy prices and hence the revenue of the British North Sea Oil Corporation. The achievement of such operating results at a time when the Government was trying to squeeze monetary demand could only be achieved through still further cuts in the investment programmes of the nationalised industries, and through increases in the prices at which the goods and services of nationalised industries were sold.

Price increases imposed by the nationalised industries are similar in their effects to higher taxes. Most people cannot avoid paying whatever price is charged for the products of the nationalised industries. The demand for electricity and gas, for posts and telephones, and for public transport, is unlikely to fall much in response to higher prices, because there are few substitutes for them. So higher charges have to be borne by the consumers of these products as best they can. In effect, "cuts" in public sector borrowing achieved by raising nationalised industries' prices are akin to higher taxes, both in the sense that, like taxes, these higher prices channel resources into the public sector, and in the sense that the people from whom they are levied have very little choice about paying them. But unlike progressive income taxes, which fall most heavily on the highest earners, increased charges hit the relatively less well off hardest.

However, higher charges for the products of the nationalised industries were only one half of the Thatcher Government's policy on State industries. The most positive aspect was the policy of "privatisation": the sale of public sector assets to the private sector. Such sales have a favourable impact on the P.S.B.R. in two ways. In the short term, they provide a once-off cash income which can be used to finance part of the public expenditure programme. In the longer term, the fact that these assets are sold to the private sector means that future borrowings against them will not affect the P.S.B.R. either. Quite apart from these narrow financial effects, privatisation has an obvious attraction to a political party committed to "free enterprise" and market economics. It directly transfers control over resources from the State back to the private sector, and in so doing it rolls back the frontiers of Government intervention in the economy.

The practical application of privatisation was embodied in a series of measures introduced by the Thatcher Government in its first eighteen months in office. The measures did not cover the sale of assets in the three large "basic" industries in which the State had significant shareholdings: coal (through the National Coal Board), steel (through the British Steel Corporation) and vehicles (through British Leyland). There was a very good reason for this. These firms were chronic loss-makers; they were therefore not attractive to the private sector. The Government's intent was instead to broaden the scope of private enterprise in the three other fields of the economy where State intervention had been significant since 1945: in communications, transport, and the provision of energy.

As far as communications were concerned, the Thatcher Government first split the Post Office into two sections. The Post Office itself retained responsibility for posts; the newly-created British Telecom took over the responsibility for telecommunications, of which telephones formed the single most important element. Telecommunications were also opened up to private competition. British Telecom lost the Post Office's traditional monopoly over the supply and maintenance of telephone equipment attached to the public network, although it retained the sole right to provide the first telephone in each household or business place.

In the public transport sector, the Government's strategy was much more directly aimed at transferring assets back to the private sector. British Rail's non-railway assets (including the Sealink shipping company and property investments) were transferred to a new holding company, which would be able to sell its shares to private investors. The British Transport Docks Board, a profitable public enterprise which owned nineteen of the nation's docks, was also empowered to sell shares to the private sector. The Transport Minister, however, gave a commitment that the Docks Board would continue to be run as a single entity in which the Government would hold a majority of shares; although it would enjoy "full commercial freedom" in its operations and not be shackled by the normal nationalised industry borrowing constraints. The Minister also pledged the sale of the shares in the National Freight Corporation, which controlled about 10 per cent of Britain's haulage business; and in the State airline, British Airways. These companies were, however, barely profitable, and therefore not immediately attractive to private investors. Even less attractive were Government's shares in its final major holding in the transport sector, British Shipbuilders, which was undertaking drastic cut-backs in its capacity and its work-force in a desperate effort to survive the slump in world shipbuilding.

If private demand for the State's assets in the transport sector was less then enthusiastic, the same cannot be said for the State's holdings in energy. In 1979 the private sector would have welcomed sales of shares in the British North Sea Oil Corporation (B.N.O.C.) with open arms. Yet the Thatcher Government, despite its manifesto commitment to do so, was reluctant to sell off B.N.O.C.'s equity to private investors. This was a case in which pragmatism triumphed over principle. Once in office, the Thatcher Government realised that a one-off sale of B.N.O.C.'s shares was unlikely to yield the revenues which could be expected to accrue through time as a result of a continuing rise in the price of oil; and it was not until 1982, when the oil price was falling as a result of international recession, that part of B.N.O.C.'s equity was sold off. There was similar resistance to the proposal to sell off British Gas's oil interests. The first significant move towards privatisation in the energy sector was the Government's decision to end the Electricity Council's monopoly in the sale of electricity to the public, and allow anyone to set up in the electricity business. Yet even in the case of this reform it was unlikely that any private investor could raise the sort of capital that would be required to build power stations and develop a grid big enough to reap the scale economies necessary to compete with the Electricity Council.

V

The consequences of the New Orthodoxy have been similar to those of the disastrous "Treasury Orthodoxy" which determined British economic policy between 1925 and 1931.

The background to the two periods was remarkably similar. In both cases, a period of economic stability had been succeeded by inflation and slump. The uncertainty had stimulated the desire for reassurance, and a demand for a return to "sound money".

The circumstances of the 1925–31 period are worth reviewing. After a long period of economic stability up to 1914, Britain had experienced a sharp inflation during the First World War – the general level of retail prices in 1920 was three times higher than it had been in 1914. After 1920, when the post-war boom had burnt itself out, Britain suffered a slump as severe as any it has ever known. Between 1920 and 1922, the rate of unemployment rose from 2 per cent to more that 14 per cent; and it still remained over 11 per cent three years later.

In an effort to regain the stability of the pre-First World War era, the Baldwin Government decided to return to the Gold Standard which had existed before 1914. Under the Gold Standard, sterling was convertible into gold at the official par value. The idea was that confidence in sterling would be restored if it was backed by a unit of "absolute" value; and gold was the most widely accepted such unit. To complete the psychological reassurance that "sound money" had been restored, the Baldwin Government chose to return to gold at the pre-1914 parity, giving an exchange-rate for sterling internationally of £1=US $4.86. Keynes at the time estimated that this was an over-valuation of some 10 per cent, and that the exchange rate which would have reflected the true relative purchasing powers of the £ and US dollar would have been £1=US $4.40.

In 1925, as in 1979, the interests of the industrial sector of the British economy were sacrificed to the financial sector. Analysing the decision to return to gold in 1925, W. Adams Brown wrote that:

> The immediate need of the export industries [in 1925] was a rate of exchange that would accurately reflect the parity between the purchasing power of the £ abroad and its purchasing power over material and labour at home. The immediate need of the London money market and the entrepot trade was a rate of exchange restricted in its fluctuations by gold points so as to provide a stable medium for the transaction of its business as financier and middleman for the trade of the world.

W. Adams Brown, in S. Pollard (ed.) *The Gold Standard and Employment Policies between the Wars*

The consequence of the triumph of the immediate needs of the London money market over those of the export industries in the decision to return to gold at $4.86 was that the competitiveness of British industry on world markets was eroded. In 1924, before Britain returned to gold, earnings from visible exports had funded 80 per cent of the nation's import requirements. Between 1925 and 1929, the proportion of imports financed by visible export earnings fell to two-thirds; and by 1931, the value of visible exports was less than half that of imports.

To maintain the value of the £ in the face of a deteriorating Balance of Trade, the Bank of England had to maintain a regime of high interest rates to induce foreigners to hold their reserves in sterling balances in London. The City of London prospered; industry was depressed.

Instead of recognising that the main proximate cause of industry's depression was an over-valued currency and high interest rates, the Baldwin Government tried to put the blame on the trade unions and attempted to reduce the wages of their members. The consequence was the General Strike of 1926, which started when the coal miners resisted a cut in their money wages. However, the defeat of the trade unions by the Government and the employers, and the passage of anti-union legislation in 1927, did not usher in a period of prosperity. Real wages remained depressed, and an atmosphere of defeat pervaded the trade union movement. Yet the employers did not benefit – the gross trading profits of companies and statutory corporations remained below 13 per cent of a national income until 1933 (this compares with a proportion of more than 17 per cent throughout the 1970s, except 1975).

Recovery did not take place until the Gold Standard had collapsed in 1931. The Wall Street crash of 1929 was followed by banking crises in continental Europe which caused many foreign holders of sterling to withdraw their money from London to cover their losses at home. In the face of these outflows, the parity of sterling could not be sustained. After the devaluation of sterling, the regime of high interest rates was no longer necessary. With cheap money and a realistically valued £, slow recovery of the British economy occurred in the 1930s. Unemployment fell from the unprecedented levels it reached in 1931–32, when it had stood at over one-fifth of the registered labour force. But with the industrial base eroded by the policies of "sound money", job creation was difficult and took a long time coming. Unemployment was never less than one in ten of the registered labour force even during the late 1930s; it only fell below this with the advent of the Second World War and the revolution in economic policy it brought with it. In the face of a direct threat to national survival, the fallacies of "sound money" were swept away.

It took thirty years for them to re-emerge; nearly forty years for them to become the dominating principles of national economic policy. Nearly two generations have passed; it is perhaps too long for the experience of 1925–31 to be remembered.

"Those who do not remember the past are condemned to relive it," in the words of Santayana.

And so in the early 1980s, manufacturing industry in Britain was once more depressed – squeezed between an over-valued currency and high interest rates on the one hand, and deflationary economic policies on the other. Industrial profitability was lower than it had been since the early 1930s, and yet real wages were not rising. Workers and employers suffered together, but those who suffered most were the men and women without a job, unwanted and without respect in their own country; forgotten sacrifices on the high altar of sound money.

The advocates of the New Orthodoxy put the blame for the depression on trade unions – the scapegoat of the Gold Standard.

In the early 1980s, as during the 1920s, the Orthodox view was that unemployment was caused by excessive real wages and that the answer was a reduction in real wages. So it is that contemporary exponents of the Orthodoxy, like Samuel Brittan, can argue that, "If there is one thing that stands out a mile, it is that employers and union leaders have connived in raising money wages and maintaining real wages in the face of market pressures at the expense of the jobless." (Samuel Brittan, *Financial Times*, 19.6.1980.) In the early 1980s, as during the 1920s, attempts to cut real wages precipitated long and bitter industrial disputes; and pressure mounted for legislation to weaken the position of the trade unions, to limit their right to strike and to picket. In the early 1980s, as during the 1920s, the Orthodox view was that inflation was caused by excessive monetary growth, to which the answer was monetary control through high interest rates in the private sector, and retrenchment in the public sector.

But at the end of the day, the New Orthodoxy of the 1980s was no more successful in stimulating economic growth, or even restoring sound money, than was the Treasury Orthodoxy of the 1920s. To appreciate why the policies of the New Orthodoxy failed it is worth recalling the judgement of the economic historian Sidney Pollard on the failure of the Gold Standard in the 1920s. "The City of London's prosperity was always based, ultimately, on Britain's industrial strength, and not the other way about. By undermining industry (particularly exports) the City cut the ground from under its own feet, in the long run." (Sidney Pollard, in S. Pollard (ed.), *The Gold Standard and Employment Policies between the Wars*.)

Like the inter-war Treasury Orthodoxy, the New Orthodoxy of monetarism sought to end inflation and restore economic stability. But, also like the Treasury Orthodoxy, its whole vision of the way the economy works was *static*; it failed to work through the implications of its policies over a period of years.

Put in its simplest terms, inflation is a condition which arises when the aggregate monetary demand of an economy outruns its capacity to produce goods. But if the means chosen to cut back monetary demand simultaneously reduce the economy's productive capacity, then the inflationary problem may perversely become worse as a result of the "anti-inflationary" measures.

In very crude terms, this is what happened in Britain. Governments of the post-1968 period concentrated on monetary *demand*, to the neglect of the supply-side of the economy. Attempts to restrict the growth of the money supply through high interest rates fell most heavily on industrial borrowers; house-buyers were protected by covert subsidies. This caused a shift of savings out of industrial investment, which increases an economy's productive capacity and its potential for income-generation, and into property, and especially residential property, which contributes to production only indirectly.

Similarly, retrenchment in the public sector fell most heavily on investment – in plant, machinery, infrastructure and education – which is necessary to maintain and expand the economy's ability to produce. This type of expenditure was regarded by the monetarists as no different from spending on defence or civil servants' salaries; and since cutbacks in capital expenditure were easier to implement than cutbacks in current expenditure, this is where they were implemented. The consequence was that the U.K. in the 1980s had an outdated and inefficient transport and communications infrastructure, which undermined the ability of its manufacturing industry to produce efficiently and to compete on world markets.

Chapter Four

TOWARDS A DYNAMIC ECONOMY

> Just as in the clock, the result of the complex action of countless different wheels and blocks is only the slow, regular movement of the hand marking the time, so the result of all the complex human movement – of all the passions, hopes, regrets, humiliations, sufferings, impulses of pride, of fear, and of enthusiasm of those men – was only . . . the slow shifting of the registering hand on the dial of the history of mankind.
>
> Tolstoy, *War and Peace* III

I

IT WAS A dictum of Napoleon that "a general will never be a great commander if he cannot see beyond his own map board".

It is not difficult for a general to look beyond his own sphere of action when a war is going well. The overall strategy is hardly likely to be in question. The general, replete in his own success, can relax with some satisfaction and discuss progress on other fronts with his advisers and fellow-officers in an atmosphere of camaraderie and mutual respect.

The true test of a general's mettle comes when the war is going badly. Then each battle is likely to be a defensive struggle against the odds, fought by soldiers whose morale is low. The general is likely to face enough problems on his own map board to keep him fully occupied. Yet if the general fails to examine the overall strategy, he runs the risk of being the leader of a defeated army.

The general is in a quandary. If he questions the overall strategy, he will be accused of failing to give his full attention to his own area of operations, and of being disloyal to the cause. If the general goes too far out on a limb, he risks being ostracised completely, and perhaps even dismissed from the Army. The line of least resistance is for the general to abstract himself from the problems elsewhere on the front, and to concentrate exclusively on his own map board:

to ensure that, whatever happens elsewhere, at least in his own sphere the tactics pursued are technically sound. If the general is successful in these limited objectives, he might be judged to have proved himself to be a good general – but not a great commander. He had neither the courage nor the vision to strike out beyond his own map board, and to put at risk his own personal future in the hope of changing the strategy by which the war was being fought.

As it is in war, so it is in politics. British politics after 1945 was blessed by many good generals, but not one great commander. During the post-war era, British Government was run by technocrats who sought to administer their own departments efficiently within the accepted social framework. This approach was successful during the years between 1945 and 1970, when Britain experienced steady growth, full employment, and negligible inflation. During that period, the underlying strategy was bringing about the desired results; and in such circumstances good generals running their own sphere of operations with competence and integrity were all that was required. But when the underlying strategy is not producing the desired results, then a nation led by politicians who are merely competent within their own specialist fields of administration is unlikely to progress. Such politicians will be more concerned with justifying their own policies than with offering a new vision of the future which provides real hope.

Perhaps it is wrong to blame the politicians alone, because the theorists upon whose ideas their policies were based offered narrow and static prescriptions for Britain's ills. As Britain's economic and social decline gathered pace after 1970, so economists and sociologists withdrew ever further from reality into the reassuring cocoon of pure theory. The assumptions from which such theory started might be ridiculous, but this seemed to be less important than that the methodology by which the conclusions were derived was logically sound and mathematically elegant. In consequence, the theorists became trapped within the cloying intricacies of their own hypothetical constructs, bounded by the self-imposed limits of their own jargon, unable to see beyond their specialities to the broad dynamics of society. They were capable of arguing about the technicalities of monetary management, or of incomes policies, but incapable of comprehending the substance behind them.

Economic theory is like a kaleidoscope, which when shaken by the external reality of historic events produces colourful patterns which seem to be new, yet show a curious similarity to the patterns of the past. On closer examination, these patterns prove to be not new at all, but merely the same pieces as before, juggled into a slightly different manner by the external shocks to which they have been subjected. So it is that the rejection of Keynesian economics has not led to any real advances in social or political thinking, but merely to the recrudescence of the failed Treasury Orthodoxy of the inter-war years in its contemporary guise as monetarism.

If anything is to be done to improve the lives of the unemployed and underprivileged, then it is necessary to break out of the static framework of orthodox economic theory. It is necessary to draw on ideas never taught in the universities, which provide an insight into the broad sweep of human history – which, to paraphrase Tolstoy, do not merely dissect a component part of the social framework as it appears in a moment of time, but seek to examine the interaction of all the component parts through time, and to discover the driving forces behind "the slow shifting of the registering hand on the dial of the history of mankind".

II

In the autumn of 1930 an obscure Russian academic called Nikolai Kondratieff was arrested by the Soviet secret police in one of Stalin's earliest purges. He was alleged to be the head of an illegal movement against the Russian Government and was deported to Siberia. His fate thereafter is unknown, but may be guessed at. Kondratieff would not today be remembered any more than the other hundreds of thousands of victims of the Stalinist purges, had it not been for a single paper he had published during the 1920s.

This paper was published in English under the title of "The Long Waves in Economic Life" in the *Review of Economic Statistics* in 1935. In it, Kondratieff made a single, straightforward observation, without attempting to develop any theory as to why it should occur. This observation was that long waves, lasting some 45–55 years each, occur in economic activity throughout capitalist economies. These waves have two main phases – an upswing, in which the level of activity of the means of production is increasing; followed by a downswing, in which it is falling. Each phase was approximately a quarter of a century in length.

The existence of this long wave, which was called the Kondratieff after the man who identified it, was not accepted by most conventional economists. There were several good reasons for this.

Firstly, even Kondratieff himself had proffered no explanation as to *why* his wave should occur; nor could any explanation be found within the confines of orthodox economics. Secondly, the number of long waves Kondratieff identified were insufficient to provide convincing proof of their existence – in the case of Britain, the world's first industrial economy, Kondratieff only identified two and a half long waves over the period 1780 to 1920. Thirdly, the statistical base on which Kondratieff sought to establish his observations was severely restricted by the data available at the time. Kondratieff used five main series to try to prove the existence of long waves: commodity prices; interest rates; money wages; foreign trade; and the physical volume of production of certain key industrial commodities such as coal, iron, and lead. Yet each of these series is influenced by many other factors apart from the real level of economic activity: for example, commodity prices and money wages are related to the total quantity of money in the economy; while the demand for particular industrial commodities like coal, iron and lead is a function of the availability and relative price of substitutes for them – and because substitutes have been successfully developed in the years since 1920, the relative demand for coal, iron and lead has fallen, quite independently of the aggregate level of economic activity. Finally, Kondratieff's findings have been criticised on the grounds that his methodology was unsound. The technique Kondratieff used to eliminate short fluctuations and random disturbances from the secular trend was a nine-year moving average. Yet the adoption of a moving average can have the effect, not merely of smoothing out a secular trend, but of actually generating cycles from a series of purely random disturbances from the mean: the so-called "Slutsky-Yule" effect.

On all these grounds, orthodox economists have been content to reject the existence of the Kondratieff wave as unproven.

Yet if the evidence is examined more closely, the case for the Kondratieff looks more convincing. First of all, it is now nearly sixty years since Kondratieff wrote his paper, and the evidence of the intervening years appears to have supported his thesis. The inter-war years were clearly a long downswing, as Kondratieff predicted in his paper; the post-war generation was the succeeding upswing; and since the late 1960s the world economy has entered a long downswing.

The proximate cause of these long waves is worth examining in a little more detail.

Since Kondratieff wrote, the concept of national income has been developed by Keynes and his disciples, and authoritative estimates of the U.K.'s national income for the years from 1855 to 1965 have been prepared by C. H. Feinstein of Cambridge University. Feinstein's statistics reveal that the component of national income showing the greatest fluctuations, whether measured in current prices or in constant terms, has been Gross Domestic Fixed Capital Formation: the aggregate amount invested in buildings, plant and equipment. The price of the finance raised to fund such investment is the rate of interest; and orthodox neo-classical economic theory teaches that, the higher the rate of interest and hence the cost of investment, the lower aggregate investment should be, other things being equal. But interestingly, Feinstein's data show that aggregate investment has fluctuated directly with the rate of interest through the long waves.

The implication is that the predominant relationship has historically run *from* the demand for investable funds *to* the rate of interest, or price of those funds – and not the other way about. High and rising interest rates have not discouraged high and rising investment in the upswing of the long wave; nor have falling real interest rates reversed a decline in investment during the downswing. Rising investment has pulled up interest rates as borrowers compete for limited investment funds, while falling investment has caused their decline.

So far, we have merely an observation, with no explanation as to why it should occur.

Nor does conventional economic theory provide any clues. The neo-classical orthodoxy postulates that the interaction of free markets should result in a stable equilibrium in the economy. Neo-classical economics has always had difficulty in explaining regular cycles in economic activity; within the framework of neo-classical analysis, disruption from equilibrium can only occur in response to a shock *from outside* the market system, from wars or natural disasters or governments which print money to finance public expenditure.

Keynesian theory has found it easier to explain medium-term business cycles by the operation of factors endogenous to the economic system. Keynesian theory can explain instability within market capitalism through the interaction of the multiplier and accelerator mechanisms; and theories incorporating these factors have been developed to explain medium-term business cycles.

However, these mechanisms cannot explain long waves which last, not a few years, but several decades.

The only economist who has yet offered a satisfactory analysis of the Kondratieff wave was a man who does not fit neatly into either the neo-classical or the neo-Keynesian schools of thought. He was an Austrian economist who emigrated to the United States, where he taught for many years as a Professor at Harvard University. His name was Joseph Schumpeter.

A century and a half separates the Classical economists of the early nineteenth century and the contemporary analysts who have revived interest in the theory of economic growth since the Second World War. During this century and a half, Joseph Schumpeter was the only major economic theorist, other than Karl Marx, to tackle seriously the question of how capitalist economies develop through time.

Like Marx, Schumpeter tried to build his theory upon a vision of how capitalist economies had actually developed in the past: that is to say, his method of approach was historical, or inductive, as opposed to the modern deductive method which attempts to derive its conclusions through the application of logic and mathematics to given assumptions. Like Marx, but unlike modern growth theorists, Schumpeter attempted to integrate economic progress, social relationships and the institutional framework of a society into a coherent whole, to form an overall vision of social development.

But here the similarity between Marx and Schumpeter ends. Schumpeter was never a socialist, nor even a social reformer. He sought merely to analyse society, not to change it. The problem to which Schumpeter addressed himself was, he later wrote, "the question of how the economic system generates the force which incessantly transforms it".

He took as his starting-point an economic system which did not change through time, but merely repeated itself period after period – a stationary state economy. He assumed that the economy was commercially organised; that is, it was one in which there was private property, division of labour, and free competition in all markets. On these assumptions, Schumpeter developed a model of the stationary state economy which was essentially an orthodox neo-classical model, in which all consumers and producers maximise their welfare, subject to the constraints placed upon them by the available technology of production and natural resources.

Schumpeter accepted that the stationary state would not be disrupted by increases in the working population or by changes in the propensity to save. He accepted that the economy could adjust smoothly to these factors without leaving equilibrium for a prolonged period.

However, the important question for Schumpeter was not whether the introduction of these factors would leave the general equilibrium stable and mathematically consistent, but whether it was these factors which had in fact revolutionised material standards of life since the Industrial Revolution. Schumpeter made his view on this issue clear in 1912:

> Different methods of employment, and not saving and increases in the available quantity of labour, have changed the face of the economic world in the last fifty years. The increase in population especially, but also of the sources from which savings can be made, was first made possible in large measure through different employment of the existing means.
>
> *The Theory of Economic Development*, ch. 2

Schumpeter's thesis was that changes in the methods of employment of the means of production were the driving-force of economic progress. He termed these changes "innovations" and postulated that innovations caused economic development. Unlike growth, which merely increases the *quantity* of goods produced by the economic system, innovation changes their *quality*, so that no comparison can be made between the amount of goods produced before and after the development process. The tools of stationary state analysis were inadequate for the study of economic development, since they could not predict the causes or effects of discontinuous changes in methods of production; but could only investigate the new equilibrium position after the changes have occurred.

Innovation does not occur spontaneously. It must be actively promoted by a human agent, whom Schumpeter called the entrepreneur. The entrepreneur carries out the function of enterprise, or of conceiving new combinations of the factors of production; and this function is quite distinct from that of routine management of the productive processes; and also from the function of the capitalist, who supplies the finance for a new project but does not necessarily participate in its organisation.

The entrepreneur needs two things to carry out an innovation: he must see the potential for an innovation, and he must be able to mobilise productive resources so as to realise that potential. In a capitalist economy, this control is vested in anyone with the ability to pay the owners of the productive resources to work for him. This ability depends on access to finance capital, which in a capitalist economy can be created by the banking system.

The banking system can build a credit structure on its reserve base, and can lend this credit to entrepreneurs. The credit borrowed by entrepreneurs is used by them to pay the productive resources employed in innovations. However, once the innovations are successfully established, and their output is being sold, the revenue earned from sales is sufficient to pay for the original inputs, repay the initial loan over time, and have something left over – entrepreneurial profits.

Entrepreneurial profits are however only a temporary phenomenon in a competitive economy. Other producers in search of profit will imitate the original innovator, and bid up the prices of the original factors as they compete for them. Conversely, the price of the final output produced by the sector tends to fall as production expands. Thus, profits are squeezed until, if no further innovation is introduced, the sector tends to return to a competitive equilibrium in which only "normal" profits are being earned; and the economy as a whole tends to return to a stationary state.

The essential link between Schumpeter's micro-economic theory of development and his macro-economic theory of trade cycles was his view that innovations tend to cluster together. Schumpeter argued that, while invention – the development of new processes at laboratory level – goes on continuously in time, innovation – the *application* of newly developed processes to commercial use – does not.

The main reason for this is that innovation requires active and successful promotion by the entrepreneur. Innovations do not happen by accident; they require effort and determination to be brought into commercial operation. But once an innovation has been successfully introduced, it becomes much easier for new producers to come into the industry in order to develop a process which is already operating successfully, and to exploit a market whose potential has already been proved.

In the case of major innovations, their successful introduction is likely to lead to many spin-offs. Thus, the construction of railroads across the United States in the mid-nineteenth century opened up unexploited sources of raw materials and agricultural land. Similarly, the railroads were necessary for the development of a nationwide postal system, and for the creation of a distribution network for the popular press. Such major innovations have formed the basis of the long waves observed by Kondratieff. They take several decades to work fully through the economic system.

It is these innovations that provide the main impetus behind the increase in investment. The investment boom in the upswing of the long wave is not caused primarily by the growth of existing production processes, but rather by the *transformation* of the economy through the emergence of new production processes which displace existing processes. For example, passenger and freight transport has not advanced over the past two hundred years because of an increase in the number of horses and carts, but rather because of successive transformations in the methods of transportation. Thus, the first long wave saw the development of canals; the second, the development of railways and steamships; the third, trams and automobiles; and the fourth, aeroplanes. In addition to the direct stimulus that investment in these sectors had on the economy, the emergence of each new form of transportation has widened the effective markets in which productive inputs and final goods are traded, and consequently given rise to a range of investment opportunities.

Schumpeter's most detailed examination of the long wave was in his monumental two-volume study, *Business Cycles*, published in 1939. In this work, Schumpeter distinguished four distinct phases in each long wave, which can be summarised as follows:

(1) The *primary upswing*, which is generated by an increase in autonomous investment to finance the introduction of a major innovation or group of innovations. The first sectors to experience an upsurge of autonomous investment may not contribute directly to the production of consumer goods, but rather provide the infra-structure for such production: embodying major advances in transport, communications, or energy. Once the first group of entrepreneurs has successfully introduced an innovation, they are in a monopoly position, and can earn monopoly profits which enable them to expand rapidly. But initially it is likely that they will

be at least partly dependent on external credit for funding their investment. The primary upswing is consequently characterised by a rising rate of profit in the leading sectors, rising real interest-rates, and an increased amount of credit creation by the banking system for lending to new enterprise. Aggregate real demand for the means of production increases as the new projects compete with existing processes for them.

(2) An innovatory boom cannot last indefinitely, because during the boom the commercial application of scientific advance occurs more rapidly than the scientific advance itself; so innovation tends to catch up with invention. However, although the potential for further innovation recedes, a *secondary upswing* in autonomous investment can be sustained. The profits being made by the original entrepreneurs attract imitators into the market, who copy, extend and improve the innovations and exploit related investment opportunities. The entry of imitators erodes the monopoly position of the original entrepreneurs, and in consequence a rising level of autonomous investment and high pressure of demand for the means of production is associated in this phase with a falling rate of profit in the innovatory sectors.

(3) Falling profit-margins caused by the entry of imitators into the market eventually undermine the impulse for autonomous investment. Without an increase in the level of autonomous investment, the rate of growth of national income and the pressure of demand for the productive factors both tend to fall. The long wave enters its *recession* phase. The crisis in the post-Second World War long wave, when the secondary upswing ended and the long wave recession began, occurred in the late 1960s (1968–69). Once the downswing of the long wave has begun, the multiplier-accelerator interaction will drive aggregate real demand below the potential capacity of the economy to supply goods. Some ventures which would have been successful if activity had been maintained may go to the wall. The climate for fresh innovation will be difficult; and credit from banks for new ventures will be tight, even though real interest rates are falling.

(4) Eventually, the recession phase reaches its lowest point, in a *Depression*, or slump. Fixed investment has fallen to its lowest point; eventually the firms remaining in operation have to replace worn-out plant and machinery and replenish their stocks. In addition, there may be a bunching of demand for consumers' durables, such as housing, purchase of which is partly credit-

financed and stimulated by low real interest rates. These factors generate the *Recovery* from Depression. A recovery is distinguished from the upswing in that it does not arise as a result of the transformation of the economy through the introduction of new techniques. Pressure of demand for the means of production increases slightly compared to the Depression, as the economy picks up from its low point. But unemployment in the labour market remains high, and the real level of interest rates remains low. Industrial profitability also remains low.

KONDRATIEFF WAVES IN THE BRITISH ECONOMY
SINCE THE INDUSTRIAL REVOLUTION

	PHASE OF THE CYCLE				
	(1) *Primary Upswing*	(2) *Secondary Upswing*	(3) *Recession*	(4) *Recovery*	Duration
(1)					
The "Industrial Revolution" Kondratieff	1787–1800	1801–13	1814–29	1830–44	58
Leading sectors – canals & shipping; coal; textiles					5
(2)					
The "Bourgeois" Kondratieff	1845–61	1862–73	1874–85	1886–97	53
Leading sectors – railroads & steamships; steam power					3
(3)					
The "Imperial" Kondratieff	1898–1908	1909–21	1922–33	1934–47	50
Leading sectors – automobiles; gas & electricity; chemicals & electrical engineering					2
(4)					
The "Space Age" Kondratieff	1948–58	1959–69	1970–83	84–96	48
Leading sectors – aerospace; radar & television; electronics					

The approximate timing of each of these phases is shown for the four Kondratieffs that Britain has experienced since the Industrial Revolution on the above Table. At the time of writing, in the early 1980s, we appear to be approaching the end of the recession phase of the fourth Kondratieff. The trough of the long wave will probably occur in 1981–82. Thereafter, there will be some recovery – but it will be a recovery such as that of the 1930s, after the depths of the Great Depression of 1929–32. Unemployment will remain high, and national income will grow only very slowly. Autonomous investment will remain stagnant, and profitability will remain depressed. In the normal course of events, a genuine secular upswing in the economy will not occur until the mid-1990s at the earliest.

Within this secular pattern, there are medium-term cyclical fluctuations, which last five to ten years on average. However, as Schumpeter pointed out in *Business Cycles*, the *character* of these medium-term cycles, which he termed Juglars after the man who first identified them, is determined by the phase of the long wave in which the economy finds itself. During the long wave upswing, the whole thrust of the economy is upwards; economic activity is buoyant; innovations are being introduced and developed; there is an autonomous impulse to invest in the private sector of the economy. Employment of the factors of production is consequently sustained at a high level throughout the shorter cycles. Short-term upswings in output and national income are strong and sustained; downswings weak and short.

By contrast, during the downswings of the long waves, the economy is stagnant. Medium-term cyclical fluctuations reflect this: short-term upswings are weak and are sustained only for one or two years; while the downswings may see an actual fall in output and national income, and not merely a slowdown in their rate of growth.

All these tendencies can be clearly seen in the medium-term cyclical fluctuations in the British economy since 1945. Fluctuations in the rate of employment, the rate of growth of Gross Domestic Product (G.D.P.), and the rate of growth of manufacturing output are shown diagrammatically on the following pages. Seven Juglar cycles are clearly identifiable, measured from trough to trough as follows:

	Cycle	Period	*Average percentage rate during the cycle of:* (1) Unemployment	(2) Growth of real G.D.P.	(3) Growth of manufacturing output
(1)	Post-war reconstruction	1946–52	2·1	2·4	6·7
(2)	The Butler boom	1952–58	1·6	2·6	3·3
(3)	The Macmillan years	1958–62	2·0	3·1	3·3
(4)	The dash for growth	1962–67	1·9	3·0	3·6
(5)	Post-devaluation restraint	1967–71	2·5	2·3	2·7
(6)	The Heath-Barber boom	1971–75	3·2	2·9	2·2
(7)	Monetarist recession	1975–83(?)	7·5 (to 1982)	0·7 (to 1981)	−1·8 (to 1982)

On Figure III, the change in the character of the Juglar cycle in Britain after 1967–68 can be clearly seen. Until the end of the 1960s, the rate of unemployment among the registered working population never rose above 3 per cent; whereas since 1970, it has never fallen below 3 per cent, apart from a brief period during the inflationary Heath-Barber boom of 1973–74. Similarly, during the long wave upswing of 1945–68, the rate of real economic growth remained positive even during years of cyclical recession; whereas since 1970 it has been negative during years of recession such as 1974–75 and 1979–81.

The most useful research on medium-term cycles in post-war Britain has been done by Professor R. C. O. Matthews. In his study of the years 1951–64, Matthews emphasised the role of stockbuilding of both consumer and producer goods in the cycle. He found that consumption of consumer durables (such as fridges, washing-machines and cars) tended to lead the economy out of recession, as consumers sought to rebuild their stocks of durable goods after a period of restraint. Although industrial stockbuilding lagged behind the growth of output following a recession, Matthews found that once a recovery was underway, producers built up their stocks very quickly in 1955, 1960, and 1964, and this tended to accelerate

Figure III

TRADE CYCLES IN THE UNITED KINGDOM
SINCE 1946

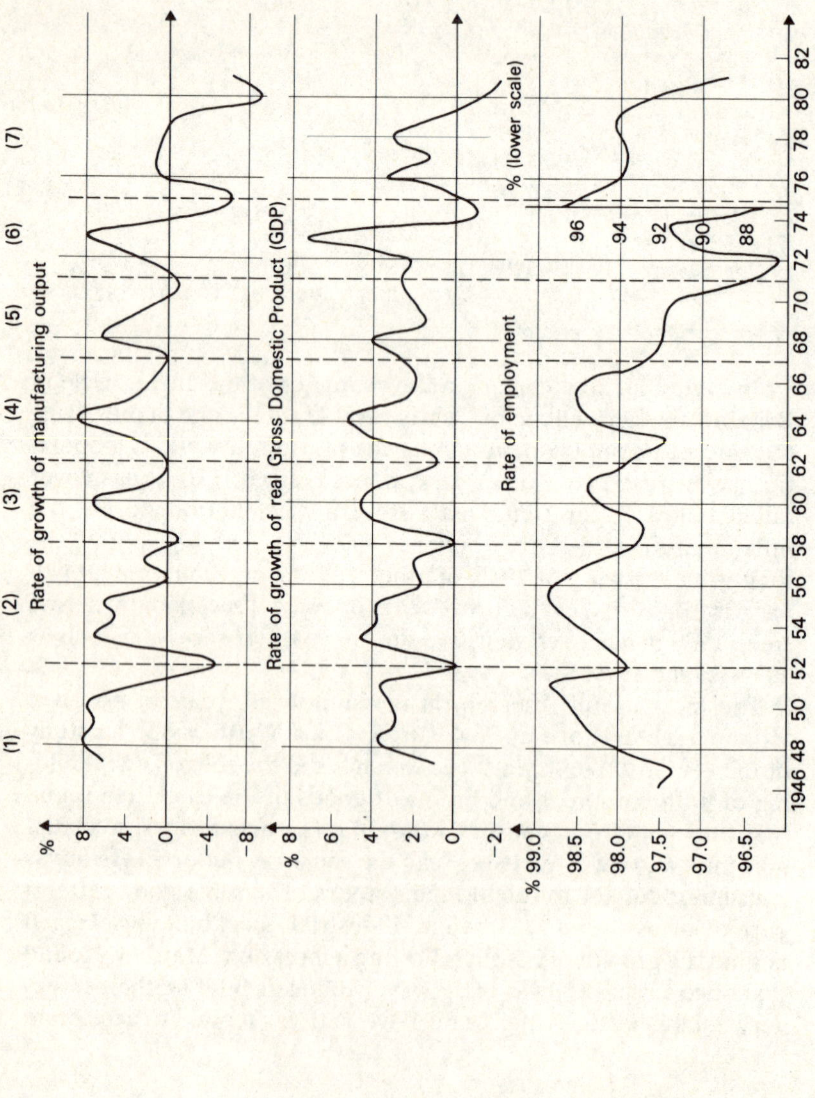

the growth in demand for final output, and to sustain the upswing of the cycle. Once producers had built up their stocks, demand for stockbuilding eased off, and the Juglar went into a down-swing. Matthews found that:

> In the immediately succeeding years (after the rapid build-up of industrial stocks) producers no longer found it necessary to maintain stockbuilding at such a high level, and a substantial decline occurred . . . at the lower turning points, fluctuations in stock-building, though considerable, have not been so violent as at the upper turning points.
>
> R. C. O. Matthews, *Postwar Business Cycles in the United Kingdom.*

Matthews also established that manufacturing investment tended to lag behind the general cycle, and his overall conclusion was that recovery from the cycle was led by consumer demand, but the course of the cycle was then amplified by the exaggerated reaction of investment demand. The general pattern thus resembled the classic multiplier-accelerator inter-action of neo-Keynesian theories of the trade cycle.

Ironically, in view of the fact that Keynesian demand management techniques were supposed to stabilise the level of economic activity, Matthews concluded they had instead tended to make cyclical fluctuations worse. He found that Government economic policy tended to hit a recession on the head, by imposing deflationary measures when the boom was already faltering. Conversely, however, Matthews found that the government may also have shortened the downswing, by reflating in time of recession, and in particular by easing restrictions on hire purchase and other forms of consumer credit, and thus encouraging the revival of demand for consumer durables earlier than might otherwise have occurred. Matthews stated that, "Government action may have increased the sharpness of year-to-year movements, but it has probably lessened the overall duration of the cycle: thus helping to account for the post-war diminution in the duration of cycles." (*Postwar Business Cycles in the United Kingdom.)*

Matthews' analysis provides the clue as to why the Juglar which started in 1975 – the seventh since the war – was longer, and the recession deeper, than any previous post-war cycle. Governments may have hit previous recessions on the head; but at least they later reflated the economy to bring it out of recession. The triumph of the new monetarist orthodoxy led the Government to deflate, not merely in the upswing, but also in the downswing. Consequently the duration of the Juglar cycle which commenced in 1975 was closer to that of pre-war cycles, which lasted on average seven to ten years, rather than post-war cycles between 1946 and 1974, which lasted between four and six years each.

The phase of the long wave explained the depth of the 1979–82 recession; while deflationary Government policies both reinforced the recession and accounted for the exceptional length of time it lasted.

Nevertheless, it would be remarkable if there was not some sort of recovery from the present slump in 1983. No doubt this recovery will be heralded by Government ministers as a triumph for the New Orthodoxy of monetarism. In fact, it will be nothing of the sort. Monetarism has not made any attempt to tackle the problems of the real economy, and has indeed contributed to those problems, by hitting hardest at investment, in both the public and private sectors of the economy. And, while monetarism may succeed in bringing down inflation, the recovery in the real economy when it comes will not be the harbinger of a new era of prosperity. Even at the peak of the next Juglar cycle – the eighth one since the War – recorded unemployment will not fall below two million; whereas even during the worst recessions of the long wave upswing of the post-war Kondratieff, unemployment never rose above half a million.

So the prospects for the 1980s are not cheerful. The rate of inflation may come down; there may be some recovery in the real economy in the mid-1980s. But there is no prospect of a genuine boom or of a return to full employment.

All this is subject to one proviso. It is that we assume the present orthodoxies remain the basis of economic policy-making.

There is hope for a better future, if the politicians can only break out of the shackles in which they are trapped by the received wisdom. If they can instead develop a clear strategy for economic growth, there is yet a chance that the 1980s will mark a return to an era of economic prosperity.

III

In 1968, one of Britain's most distinguished economists, R. C. O. Matthews, published a paper in the *Economic Journal* entitled "Why has Britain had Full Employment since the War?" In answering the question he had posed, Professor Matthews rejected the Keynesian conventional wisdom of the time. Full employment had not, he argued, been a consequence of demand management by Government. On the contrary, Government's impact on the economy had actually been deflationary: since the Second World War, the Government's budgetary surplus had averaged 3 per cent of national income each year. Matthews' conclusion was that the force underlying Britain's post-war full employment had been a sustained investment boom, and the engine which had generated this boom had been technical progress and the opportunities this had offered for profitable projects in the private sector.

Even as Matthews wrote, the long post-war investment boom was coming to an end. Gross investment in Britain had grown at an average rate of more than 6 per cent each year in real terms in the years between 1946 and 1968, so that by 1968 the annual level of investment was more than three times as great as it had been in the immediate post-war years: at £18·8 thousand million (at constant 1975 prices), compared with £6 thousand million in 1948.

But after 1968, this rapid growth ended. In 1980, the value of gross domestic fixed capital formation in constant (1975) prices was only £20·8 thousand million, compared to £18·8 thousand million twelve years earlier. Thus, whereas actual investment had trebled in real terms between 1948 and 1968, it increased by only a tenth between 1968 and 1980.

The pattern is shown graphically on the following page.

Investment is spending on buildings, plant and machinery: commodities which do not directly satisfy consumer demand, but which constitute the means by which consumer goods are produced. A slowdown in the rate of investment therefore implies that the growth of consumer goods production will also slow down. This slowdown is precisely what happened. Britain's manufacturing output was lower in 1982 than it had been in 1968.

The decline in Britain's manufacturing base has been particularly severe since the quadrupling of oil prices in 1974. Britain's

Figure IV

THE GROWTH OF GROSS DOMESTIC FIXED CAPITAL FORMATION IN CONSTANT (1975) PRICES, 1948–1981

Source: CSO, "Economic Trends", 1982, Table 14

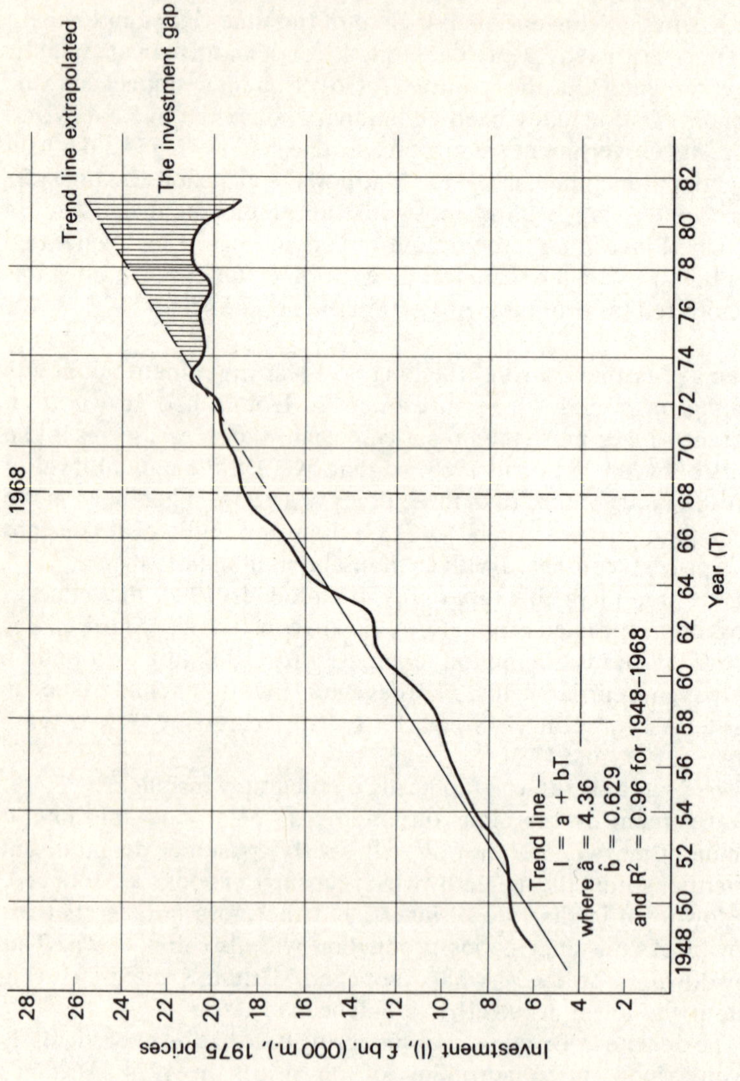

manufacturing output had grown continuously between the end of the Second World War and the early 1970s; but it then fell during the years after 1973. By the end of the 1970s, the index of manufacturing production in Britain was 5 per cent below its peak level of seven years earlier, and showed no signs of revival. Without economic growth, the era of consensus politics crumbled. Economic stagnation intensified competition between different groups over the distribution of the nation's declining resources. At its flash-points, this competition sometimes erupted into violence.

The end of the era of economic growth had two further consequences.

Firstly, it made the problem of inflation more intractable. Inflation is a condition which arises when the growth of monetary demand outstrips the growth of output. In an economy where industrial output (excluding oil) declined, it became more difficult to absorb any given level of monetary demand.

The second consequence of economic stagnation was an increase in the number of people unemployed. Without economic growth, unemployment rose inexorably, because the new jobs necessary to give opportunities to school-leavers were not created.

Neither inflation nor unemployment can be easily reduced until sustained economic growth is achieved. It is possible to estimate the approximate rate of economic growth that is required if the rate of unemployment in the U.K. is to fall. The rate of economic growth must be at least as great as the rate of growth of the effective labour-force. If it is lower than this, the economy will simply not absorb the new entrants to the labour market.

The growth of the effective labour-force is equal to the increase in the number of individuals able and willing to work, plus the increase in output per man. In the years 1960–80, the working population of Great Britain rose by an average of 0·4 per cent per annum, while productivity (or output per man) rose by just under 2½ per cent per annum. So the rate of growth of the effective labour force in Britain – the sum of these two rates – was approximately 3 per cent a year. If the rate of growth of real national income is not maintained at 3 per cent p.a. or more, then unemployment will rise.

This conclusion is borne out by the actual record of the post-war period. In fourteen of the thirty-three years between 1947 and 1979, the rate of growth of real national income was greater than 3 per cent, and in ten of those fourteen years, the rate of unemployment fell. Conversely, of the nineteen years when the rate of growth of real national income was less than 3 per cent, the rate of unemployment rose in fourteen. The relationship between economic growth and unemployment was not a linear one: if the rate of unemployment was already low, then faster growth had less impact than if unemployment was high. Yet the relationship between the rate of economic growth and the change in the numbers out of work clearly existed. So the target is defined. As the 1980s began, real national income in Britain had to grow by a minimum of 3 per cent each year if the secular rise in the numbers out of work was to be arrested; and it had to grow even faster if unemployment was to be reduced

It may be objected that it is easy enough to lay down a target like this, but impossible to achieve it.

So the first point that needs to be emphasised is that British Governments *have never made the rate of economic growth one of their prime targets*.

There was a brief period when economic growth was high on the political agenda – when the Maudling boom of 1963–64 was succeeded by an attempt by the first Wilson Government to devise a National Plan in 1965–66. But the National Plan was effectively killed in July, 1966, when a deflationary package was introduced in an abortive effort to keep down the volume of imports and maintain the parity of the £ sterling.

However, apart from this four-year period between 1963 and 1966, economic growth never figured highly on the list of priorities of post-war British Governments. During the Keynesian era, between the Second World War and the early 1970s, the main targets of economic policy were high employment and Balance of Payments equilibrium. The Keynesian approach to economic policy-making gave way during the 1970s to monetarism, whose primary objective was the reduction of the rate of inflation, through the control of the money supply, at the expense of higher unemployment and negative growth.

The central thesis of this book has been that Britain's inflationary problem, and more recently its problem of rising unemployment, are *consequences* of its slow rate of economic growth. Therefore, attempts to deal with them without tackling the underlying problem of slow growth are unlikely to enjoy anything more than merely temporary success.

The most coherent strategy to achieve a sustained growth in

national income has been developed by the economists of the Cambridge Economic Policy Group under Professor Wynne Godley: the so-called New Cambridge School. The New Cambridge School is basically Keynesian in its approach. Like Keynes during the inter-war years, the New Cambridge School is critical of the policies of demand deflation intended to restore confidence in the monetary system. Like Keynes, the New Cambridge economists argue that the multiplier effects of deflation will cause a vicious circle of decline. Thus, in their 1980 Economic Policy Review, the Cambridge Economic Policy Group argued that "Gross Domestic Product, so far from rising after this year, would continue its absolute decline. The tax base would contract, public expenditure would be forced up, and instead of there being money for tax cuts, the Government would have to raise taxes, charges and nationalised industry prices, round after round." This forecast contrasted strongly with the 1980 forecasts of the Treasury itself, and of monetarist centres such as the London Business School and the University of Liverpool, which predicted that a recovery from the recession would occur before unemployment went much above two million. The fact that the Cambridge Economic Policy Group's forecast proved all too accurate, while those of the Treasury and the monetarist universities were grossly optimistic, provides one powerful reason for believing that the Cambridge analysis is at any rate no worse than the analyses of the monetarists.

But what is more important than the Cambridge Group's analysis of what has happened and why, is its proposals as to what can be done to improve the situation, and bring the economy out of the vicious circle of decline. The Cambridge Group advocate a government-induced demand expansion as the means of achieving a real growth in national income. However, they are alive to the dangers of demand expansion unsupported by any other policies. The evidence of the post-war era, and particularly of the last major demand expansion of the Heath Government in the early 1970s, indicated that the most rapid response to demand expansion would be an increase in imports and an acceleration in the rate of domestic inflation. Domestic production would expand – if at all – only after a considerable time-lag.

The New Cambridge economists argue that the cause of this response is that producers do not immediately increase their capacity to produce goods when demand for those goods expands.

Typically, firms will run down their stocks, and attempt to work existing capacity more intensively to meet greater market demand. Firms are unlikely to undertake a permanent increase in capacity (involving a large capital outlay which can be recouped only over a period of years) unless they are confident that the higher level of demand will be sustained.

Because of the quite rational caution of producers before committing themselves to further investment in the face of rising demand, the New Cambridge economists argue that it would be necessary to maintain any expansion in aggregate demand for at least four to five years in order to bring about an increase in investment. This in turn requires that the immediate impact of demand expansion – drawing in imports and pulling up the domestic price-level – is choked off so that the expansion is not undermined.

One response to an increase in the volume of imports caused by domestic demand expansion would simply be to allow it to happen, and accept the subsequent depreciation in the exchange-rate. The problem with a devaluation is that it increases the costs of imports immediately, yet the relative demand for imports falls only after a lag. Thus, the econometricians Junz and Rhomberg estimated that the impact of devaluation might take as long as five years to work fully through. The process is described by the observed "J-Curve" in the Balance of Payments of an economy after a currency depreciation: its Balance of Payments first gets worse because the cost of its imports increases more rapidly after the devaluation than the volume of its exports; but as markets respond to the change in relative prices, more domestically-produced goods are purchased, while the volume of imports is cut back. The Balance of Payments thus traces a J-pattern in response to a devaluation: getting worse initially, but then gradually improving.

However, the Balance of Payments only improves permanently if domestic prices have been held back to enable the competitive advantage given to domestic producers through devaluation to be maintained. The immediate impact of devaluation is to increase the prices of imports, and in particular the prices of basic necessities. Increases in the prices of necessities put upward pressure on wages, as workers seek higher wages to maintain their real living-standards. The New Cambridge School adopt a wage-push theory of inflation, and argue that if there is upward pressure on wages, this will in turn cause upward pressure on domestic prices and erode the competitive advantage bestowed by inflation. If an economy responds to an increase in domestic prices by allowing a further currency depreciation it may become trapped in a vicious circle of a continuously rising level of wages and a depreciating currency.

The New Cambridge School's answer is to impose import controls. They argue that import controls will choke off imports directly, and give time for the long-term benefits of devaluation to be realised. In the 1980 Cambridge Economic Policy Review which has already been cited, import controls were proposed as part of a tripod of policies which would permit a sustained expansion in domestic demand permanently to reduce the level of unemployment. This tripod comprised devaluation, incomes policy and a comprehensive system of import controls.

Devaluation would give a once-off shift in the balance of comparative advantage from foreign to home producers. Incomes policy would prevent this advantage from being undermined by upward pressure on wages at home. Import controls would help domestic producers to withstand foreign competition during the critical period in which they would invest in additional productive capacity to exploit the advantage given by devaluation. Together, the three policies would allow Government to reflate domestic demand without the risk that it would only result in domestic inflation and a foreign exchange crisis.

The particular combination offered by the Cambridge Economic Policy Group in their 1980 Review was a 20 per cent devaluation in sterling; an incomes policy similar to that implemented in 1977 in real terms; and import controls through a comprehensive structure of tariffs, proposed at 20 per cent for semi-manufactured goods, 30 per cent for finished manufactures, and 15 per cent for services; with food, oil and raw materials having a zero tariff.

The policies offered by the New Cambridge School provide a clear alternative to those of the monetarist orthodoxy. They offer an alternative both in the tools of economic policy which are advocated, and more importantly in the objectives which those tools are designed to achieve. While the objective of the monetarists is the reduction of the rate of inflation, the New Cambridge School puts greatest emphasis on the reduction of the level of unemployment. At a time when the level of unemployment is higher than it has been at any time since the Second World War, the relevance of the strategy developed by the New Cambridge School is increasing.

However, the historic record of the policies put forward by the

Cambridge Economic Policy Group indicates that they may not of themselves be sufficient to stimulate a sustained growth in the economy.

Firstly, devaluation. It does give domestic producers a once-off advantage in world markets; but it does not guarantee that they will put that advantage to good purpose. The evidence of Britain's previous post-war devaluations in 1948, 1967 and 1972 is that they did little to stimulate greater investment and growth.

The New Cambridge economists recognise that devaluation alone is not sufficient. Yet the policies they offer to supplement it are of dubious merit. The historical evidence concerning incomes policies indicates that they have not worked, and have caused many more problems than they have solved. Indeed, it may be concluded that incomes policies *cannot* work in normal times, any more than can any form of rationing. Rationing, of which incomes policy is only one form, works only when there is a consensus on the part of those rationed that the ration is both necessary and fair. Such a consensus may emerge in time of national emergency, such as during the Second World War. But this sort of consensus has emerged only once, briefly, in peacetime, during the 1975–78 period. It is unlikely that such a consensus will emerge again for any length of time.

Nor is the experience of tariffs and import controls such as to inspire confidence in them. Political pressure for import controls has increased during every period of depression in Britain since the Industrial Revolution. This pressure has come from those hit hardest by the depression, who have justified their demands by arguing that protection is necessary to stimulate the domestic economy. However, the evidence indicates that, when it has been introduced, protection has not stimulated the domestic economy but merely enabled the protected groups to survive and transferred resources from the rest of the economy to them.

Thus, in 1828 the Corn Laws were enacted to protect domestic agriculture. They resulted in higher food prices without any compensating increase in efficiency; and by the 1840s they were discredited. Nevertheless, during the depression phase of the next long downswing in the economy, in the 1880s, pressure for protection of home industry revived in the form of the "Fair Trade" movement. This was developed by Joseph Chamberlain into the imperial preference policy which was put forward by the Conservative and Unionist Party as the main plank of their 1905 General Election campaign, when it was decisively rejected. When the economy experienced its next major downswing, in the inter-war years, demands for protection again increased. Tariffs were introduced in the 1930s, but their adoption in Britain and among her major trading partners is now recognised as an important contributory factor in the persistence of the Great Depression, when trade would otherwise have revived.

Protection will not of itself result in an economic recovery, and may actually be a contributory factor in the persistence of a recession. Where protection may have a useful function to perform is as a temporary measure, to give the economy a breathing-space in which policies can be introduced to restructure it. If this opportunity is exploited, then a modest degree of protection such as that advocated by the Cambridge Economic Policy Group may enable the economy to attain a higher level of activity and trade than would have occurred without protection.

But protection can only be a supplementary measure. The main motive-force behind a sustained growth in national income must come from investment, and particularly innovatory investment in new techniques.

IV

The first prerequisite for a growth in investment is a flow of funds to the entrepreneurs who undertake it. In Britain, there is evidence that severe distortions exist in the flow of investment funds. The Report of the Wilson Committee on Britain's financial institutions, which was published in 1980, concluded that the flow of investment funds had been affected by two factors: inflation and the growth of large institutions. Inflation, and more particularly fluctuations in it, gives rise to uncertainty regarding the returns to investment. Consequently, companies are cautious and may miss investment opportunities they would take up in more stable times. Inflation also sets a bias against long-term lending, so that projects with a lengthy pay-off period find it especially difficult to attract finance. The growth of large institutions, such as life assurance and pension funds, has tended to reinforce this bias. Because the institutions are trustees of the savings of private individuals, they tend to be timid investors: putting their money into the larger blue-chip companies, and making it harder for smaller companies to raise equity finance. Together, the growth of large institutions and the experience of endemic inflation has made it harder to raise finance for innovatory projects with long lead-times, particularly if those projects are being promoted by small firms.

The Wilson Committee saw these two factors as minor pieces of grit in an otherwise well-oiled machine. In fact, they were fundamental weaknesses. Small firms with innovatory projects are the seed-corn of future growth, and if the financial institutions are incapable of funding this sort of activity adequately, it constitutes a major obstacle to economic development.

This point was forcibly made shortly after the publication of the Wilson Committee Report by Harold Lever and George Edwards, in a series of articles they wrote for the *Sunday Times*. They compared the funding of industry by banks in the U.K. unfavourably to bank funding in Japan and West Germany. They criticised British banks for being too cautious, both in the length of time and the terms on which they lend.

> In Japan, bank loans to business amounted to something like 15 per cent of the national product between 1974 and 1978. In West Germany, the comparable figure is 8 per cent. In Britain, it is as low as 3 per cent. Japan's industrialists have really long-term loans of 15–20 years. In Germany, the formal term averages 7 years, and in Britain the formal term averages 2½ years. . . . If only a small part of savings is channelled to investment, as it is in Britain, we are not merely guaranteeing a low rate of investment, but also a high rate of unemployment and inflation.
>
> Lever and Edwards, *Sunday Times*, 2.11.80

The somewhat smug response of the bankers to this attack was that the banks were only too willing to finance industrial investment, but were not being presented with the projects.

The flood of indignant letters from industrialists to the *Sunday Times* which followed the bankers' defence indicated that this was rather less than the whole truth. The correspondence revealed that, although the banks might be fulfilling their role in funding mature, long-established quoted companies, there was unquestionably a gap in bank lending to younger private companies – particularly those seeking to introduce genuine innovations for which the market had not been tested.

As to what could be done to alter the situation, the proposals were manifold. A minority of the Wilson Committee recommended the establishment of a Small Firm Investment Company, with initial funds of £2,000m., of which half would come from the tax revenues raised on North Sea oil, and half from the institutions. Lever and Edwards, in their *Sunday Times* articles, proposed a government-backed loan guarantee scheme for small firms, by which 75 per cent of the value of bank loans to small fiirms would be guaranteed in the event of loss.

A pilot loan guarantee scheme along the lines proposed was subsequently introduced in June 1981, and to date has proved a qualified success. The pilot scheme provided a government guarantee for 80 per cent of all qualifying loans, up to a maximum of £75,000; so that if the business failed, the bank which had lent to it was liable for only 20 per cent of the bad debt. The response of small firms was far greater than anticipated: the original allocation of £150m., intended to last for three years, was all committed within twelve months, and a further allocation of £150m. was immediately brought forward. Against this, however, it was estimated that by early 1983, between 5 per cent and 20 per cent of the businesses which had borrowed under the scheme had failed or were going to fail. Nevertheless, the scheme has been a cost-efficient means of creating jobs; it has made a contribution towards plugging a very serious gap in investment financing in Britain; and it should be continued and established on a permanent basis.

More generally, the whole framework of taxation on savings needs to be overhauled, to end the bias against direct investment in companies by individuals. The large institutions have grown in large part because of the special reliefs which exist in Britain for retirement premiums and pension contributions; with the result that they now own more than half of the shares of companies quoted on the London Stock Exchange. Personal savings have been channelled into housing, because of the tax allowances offered on mortgage interest.

The relief offered for interest payments on loans to purchase a home cost the British Treasury an estimated £1·4 billion in the 1979/80 financial year, or approximately £250 per mortgage-holder. Yet it had little beneficial effect. It was inequitable: the biggest subsidies went to the rich, because mortgage tax relief was given on the top slice of a home owners' income, while the poor did not benefit from mortgage tax relief at all because they could not afford mortgages. Not only was the relief inequitable, it was also inflationary. It encouraged those who were able to do so to spend as much as possible on housing. The evidence of the 1970s was that in inflationary times, higher mortgage costs were more than outweighed by the combined impact of higher tax relief and large tax-free gains in the value of most houses: because housing, unlike holdings of industrial shares, was not subject to capital gains tax unless it was held as an investment. The consequence was that the proportion of personal wealth held in the form of housing increased from less than one-fifth in 1960, to over one-third by the end of the 1970s: a higher proportion than in any other western country.

But the real condemnation of the system of housing tax reliefs was that it did not achieve its major objective: it did not increase the number of houses built, or improve the quality of the housing stock. During the 1970s, the number of new houses built each year steadily declined; and the tax relief for house purchases, which increased money demand for housing, was soaked up by a tripling of the average price of housing.

If the government were serious about improving the housing stock, then some of the money saved by phasing out mortgage tax relief should be used to build more and better houses: a far more direct and effective means of improving people's homes than the clumsy system of subsidies presently in operation. The balance of the savings could be channelled into industrial investment.

The creation of a more favourable financial environment for industrial investment will help to stimulate Britain's recovery. But it is not sufficient on its own to bring about a return to full employment. We are presently in the downswing of the long wave, and can expect no major innovatory investment boom in the private sector until the mid- or late-1990s. Moreover, if a boom is to occur even then, it requires the development of a suitable infrastructure.

Historically, the development of the transport, communications and energy network has been a condition for an innovatory boom throughout the economy. In the eighteenth century, the construction of canals linked ports with inland towns to form regional markets and provide new arteries for trade. In the nineteenth century, the development of railways, made possible by innovations in steam power, revolutionised the transport network and opened up previously unexploited tracts of land. In the twentieth century, the development of cars and aeroplanes united different economies into a world market; advances in telecommunications permitted virtually instantaneous transmission of information around that market; and cheap fossil fuels provided industry with the source of power it required in order to exploit the vast opportunities offered.

But the age of cheap energy based on fossil fuels is now over. A new infrastructure needs to be created which has the potential of being based on renewable resources of energy. The Government must initiate the development of the economy's infrastructure. The governments of the 1970s and early 1980s were restrained from undertaking such a development programme by the inability of the monetarist orthodoxy to distinguish between borrowing to meet current expenditure, and borrowing to finance investment.

The distinction between the two types of borrowing is fundamental. If a private individual or firm borrows to cover recurrent expenses, they will eventually go bankrupt. When the public sector borrows to meet its recurrent expenses, it cannot go bankrupt; instead it covers that borrowing either by drawing savings from the private sector, where they may be used more productively; or by printing money, which may generate inflation.

But if borrowing is undertaken to finance *investment*, the situation is rather different. This is because the benefits from investment accrue over a period of years in the future. To try to finance new investment wholly from the proceeds of current and historic earnings is therefore inefficient and likely to mean investment will be sub-optimal. This is recognised in the private sector, where individuals borrow a substantial proportion of the costs of house purchase, and companies borrow to finance purchases of plant and equipment.

In the public sector, the distinction between borrowing to cover increases in current spending, and borrowing to finance viable investment projects, is not made. Both are lumped together in the "Public Sector Borrowing Requirement". Yet the two forms of borrowing are quite different in their effects. While borrowing to cover current spending is inflationary, borrowing to finance viable investment is not inflationary in the same way, because successful capital investment increases the economy's capacity to produce goods to absorb extra monetary demand.

Largely on account of their failure to make this essential distinction, British Governments of the 1970s sought to cut back the Public Sector Borrowing Requirement mainly through the reduction of capital expenditure rather than current expenditure. In so doing, they eroded the British economy's productive capacity which actually *worsened* the secular problem of inflation. Britain's failure to maintain and update the capital stock in most sectors meant that the British economy had less capacity to meet any given level of monetary demand at the beginning of the 1980s than at the beginning of the 1970s.

The approach the Government should now adopt is the reverse of that it adopted during the 1970s and early 1980s. That is to say, it should seek to hold back current expenditure while pushing forward with a major capital works programme. This programme should be directed towards converting Britain's industrial infrastructure to one that is not dependent on fossil fuels as its primary source of fuel.

It may be objected that the investment projects necessary to do this simply do not exist. But this is not the case. Several viable projects have been shelved, because of the Government's misplaced desire to reduce the Public Sector Borrowing Requirement by any means it can.

The Government has held back projects in the transport sector. British Rail has been keen for some time to push on with an electrification programme, but has been hampered by the cash constraints placed on it by the Government. Britain has the least electrified railway network of any Western European economy. At the end of the 1970s, only one-fifth of the British railway network was electrified. British Rail proposed to rectify this by extending electrification to major long-distance routes, and by introducing the electric Advanced Passenger Train to replace the existing diesel stock. The Advanced Passenger Train would reduce energy costs by nearly a third compared to diesel trains, and its maintenance costs would also be lower. Moreover, diesel trains will always of necessity be dependent on oil; an electrified network at least has the potential of being powered by other forms of energy, as these are developed. The beneficiaries of railway electrification would be the passengers and private industry, which would have access to a cheaper, quicker and more reliable means of transport.

The British Government has also slowed down its road-building programme. In particular, proposals to build ring-roads around London, Birmingham and Manchester have been put into cold storage. Yet these roads would reduce the energy costs of road freight, and the social costs of congestion.

A third project in the transport sector worth implementing is the proposed Channel Tunnel, linking Britain with the Continent. This has been under consideration for many years, and studies made of it indicate that it is a viable proposition. One proposal is for a one-track railway tunnel, costing approximately £800m., with an economic rate of return estimated by Coopers & Lybrand at between 16 and 18 per cent. Now, at a time of economic recession, with unemployed resources of skilled manpower and technical know-how, would be the best time to get this project moving.

It is not only the transport sector whose development has been held back by the straitjacket of the monetarist orthodoxy. Telecommunications have also suffered. The telecommunications sector is one of the most important growth sectors in Britain today, yet because of the limits placed by Government on British Telecom's ability to raise cash externally, the only way in which the funds can be generated for the required expansion of the system is by higher charges on existing customers – who thereby bear the cost of new services which will benefit future users.

Finally, and most crucially, the British Government has to invest more on developing alternative sources of industrial power to oil. Greater research and development are essential if the technology of generating electricity from renewable natural resources is to advance, and the costs of generation from these sources is to fall. At present, less than one-thirtieth of the Department of Energy's R & D budget is spent on research into the generation of power from the wind, the tides, and the sun; whereas over half of the Department's R & D spending is directed to nuclear power. This imbalance must be redressed.

Nevertheless, in spite of its low priority, R & D on renewable resources of energy has already produced some interesting results. One promising project is the proposal to build a tidal barrier across the Severn Estuary, costing some £5·6 billion, according to the Report of a Committee under Sir Hermann Bondi published in 1981. It has been proved feasible to build a system with two tidal basins, using both the ebb and flow of the tide to drive the generators, and this system could start producing power well before the completion of the whole project.

As a package, these projects to develop transport, telecommunications and energy would entail an investment outlay of some £2 billion a year. They would help British industry directly, by reducing the costs of its transport, communications and electric power; and they would also stimulate it indirectly, by generating additional business.

The cost of the investment programme would not represent an equivalent increase in the money supply. If the investment programme cost £2 billion a year, this would not represent an addition of £2 billion to the Public Sector Borrowing Requirement. Firstly, each extra man employed as a result of the programme would save the Exchequer about £5,000 a year (1982 prices), according to the estimates of the Manpower Services Commission. This is made up of a saving of at least £1,500 in unemployment or supplementary benefit which the Exchequer would otherwise have to pay; a net addition of £2,500 to the Exchequer's revenue in extra taxes and national insurance contributions from the newly-employed worker; and a saving of £1,000 in other benefits and administrative costs. Secondly, some of these projects would be able to mobilise funds from external sources, available to Government but not to the private sector. Thirdly, their implementation would have a multiplied effect, by creating business for the private sector and increasing the overall level of economic activity: and jobs would thereby be created in addition to those on the projects themselves. This would further reduce the financial burden of unemployment carried by the Government.

This package is by no means definitive. What is more important than the specific projects which have been suggested, are the general principles which lie behind them.

Those principles may be summed up as follows. The first priority of economic policy should be to attain a real rate of growth which is sufficient to absorb the natural increase in the effective working population. The key instrument in the attainment of this objective is the amount of investable funds the economy has at its disposal, and more importantly the use to which they are put. Where there are deficiencies or distortions in the flow of investment funds within the private sector, the Government must intervene to correct them. In addition, the Government must supplement and reinforce the private sector, particularly by the development and maintenance of an efficient infrastructure.

The pace of the Government's own capital works programme should be determined by reference to private sector activity. In the present depressed economic conditions, real investment should be increased by at least 10 per cent a year; and if the private sector is not achieving such an increase, then the Government must step up its own investment programme.

Having determined the required size of the public sector's investment programme, the rest of the Government's economic policy should follow. The Public Sector Borrowing Requirement will be determined, once an estimate can be obtained of the Government's likely success in holding down its recurrent expenditure. The funding of the Public Sector Borrowing Requirement can then be planned, which in turn will depend on the monetary policy the Government wishes to pursue, and on the real rate of economic growth.

It should be noted that this approach stands monetarism on its head. Instead of the Government's monetary policy determining its investment programme, its investment programme determines its monetary policy. Monetarism has failed to control the money supply, essentially because its implementation has reinforced a recession in the real economy. Conversely, the adoption of an economic policy targeted towards the achievement of a higher real rate of growth would reduce the pressure on the money supply, because it would reverse the trends which have caused distress borrowing.

Initially, the public investment programme might have to be financed in part by an increase in the money supply. What is important is not the size of the increase in the money supply, but the application of the increase. If the extra money is spent on projects which increase and qualitatively change productive capacity, then once the projects are operational they will repay the original investment and a process of auto-deflation will take place, causing a contraction in the money supply. Once a full programme is underway, the surplus earned from projects whose implementation is complete and which are generating benefits will offset the capital outlays on new projects coming into the implementation stage. Only if the rate of project implementation is increasing will additional sources of finance outside the programme have to be found.

Epilogue

BRITAIN AT THE CROSSROADS

I

IT IS NOW time to pull together the themes running through this book.

The inter-war years were years of waste, with more than one in ten of Britain's working population condemned to enforced idleness. The waste of the inter-war years was a loss for the whole nation, which was poorer because men and women who could have been gainfully employed producing goods and services were instead left without employment. Unemployment was a tragedy for the individuals affected, who were sentenced to a life of futility and frustration, unable to support a family properly or to build for the future.

The scourge of unemployment was banished during the Second World War. The paramount need in wartime was for national survival, and every available resource had to be mobilised towards this end. And despite all the hardships of war, despite the fact that Britain's national income was reduced by the diversion of resources to the war effort, the incidence of poverty and disease actually fell because of a fairer distribution of the limited resources available through a system of controls and rationing.

It was not market capitalism that conquered poverty and unemployment, but rather the greater regulation of the economy forced upon the government by the exigencies of war. Sir William Beveridge pointed out in 1942 that, "Want could have been abolished before the present war by redistribution of income within the wage-earning classes, without touching any of the wealthier classes. . . . Abolition of want just before the war was easily within the economic resources of the community; want was a needless scandal due to not taking the trouble to prevent it." (*Social Insurance and Allied Services*.)

By 1950, Want and the other four Giants that Beveridge had seen standing on the Road to Reconstruction – Squalor, Ignorance,

Disease, and Idleness – were largely conquered by the completion of two revolutions which had begun during the war. The first was the Keynesian Revolution in economic policy. In place of the Treasury Orthodoxy of the inter-war years, which had advocated balanced budgets and retrenchment of public spending, Keynes advocated high spending in the public sector, combined with low interest-rates to encourage investment in the private sector, as the means of maintaining full employment of resources.

Alongside the revolution in economic policy, there was a second, related revolution in social policy, which directed high public spending to the groups most in need in society, through the creation of a Welfare State. The Welfare State had three main elements: firstly, a social security system, which guaranteed everyone a minimum income from the cradle to the grave; secondly, a National Health Service, which ensured that all citizens enjoyed adequate health treatment, irrespective of their income; and thirdly, an ambitious council housing programme, whose objective was the provision of decent homes for the whole population.

With these revolutions, Beveridge's five giants were vanquished. Idleness was conquered by the adoption of a Keynesian economic policy, geared to the maintenance of full employment. Want was largely overcome by the steady family incomes generated by full employment, supplemented by a comprehensive social security system. Squalor was ameliorated by the housing programme. Disease was reduced by the establishment of the National Health Service. And Ignorance was diminished by the extended provision of State education initiated by the Butler Education Act of 1944.

Nor were these advances significantly undermined by the election of a Conservative Government in 1951, which broadly accepted the new post-war order. Thus by the mid-1950s, Anthony Crosland, in his book *The Future of Socialism*, could offer an optimistic vision of a society where the problem of economic hardship would soon be conquered, without the State taking over the commanding heights of the economy. Crosland argued that the key objective of socialism in the future would not be nationalisation, but rather "the concern with social welfare, and the desire for an equal and classless society". The economic framework was taken as given, with control over financial and industrial capital remaining in private hands. No attempt was made by either Conservative or Labour governments to alter the pattern of ownership or control over capital, or even to extend public intervention by greater planning. The Conservative Party saw the function of government in the economy as that of a referee, whose job it was to hold the ring and ensure fair play, while the allocation of resources was left to the interaction of buyers and sellers in the market. The Labour Party advocated greater social equality, but the triumph of the Revisionist wing of which Anthony Crosland was the most articulate spokesman led it to accept the existing structure of society.

The fundamental weakness of Revisionism was that its principal end, of greater equality, was contradictory with the framework it accepted, of a regulated market economy. The workings of the free market of necessity give rise to inequalities, which cannot be eradicated by a social security system built on the liberal principle of insurance. Such a system does not cause a redistribution of income from rich to poor, but merely smooths the flow of income within the life-cycle of individual families.

As a result, no significant inroads were made into the unequal distribution of wealth in Britain. At the end of the 1960s, the top one-twentieth of Britain's population still owned well over half of all personal wealth; while the bottom four-fifths of the population owned between them less than a sixth of personal wealth.

The inevitable consequence was that, when the era of sustained economic growth came to an end, the burden of decline was borne by those most in need: the very people who were least able to bear it. The wealthy élite continued to live comfortably; it was those at the bottom of the social heap who became victims of the rise in unemployment during the 1970s. And with the rise in unemployment, the weakness of the Beveridge system of social security became manifest. The principle of insurance – that the beneficiaries of the system should draw from it only to the extent that they contributed – had worked reasonably well during the era of full employment, when virtually all able-bodied men of working age made regular contributions to the national insurance scheme. But with the rise in unemployment, the proportion of people paying into the scheme fell, while the proportion drawing on it rose. The scheme inevitably went into deficit. Worse still, the numbers of people not covered by it rose, because the long-term unemployed were unable to make contributions, since they did not earn an income. They fell out of the insurance system and into the net of supplementary benefit, which Beveridge had envisaged would hold only a tiny fraction of the most unfortunate members of society. Supplementary benefit was paid only at subsistence level; and when it was drawn by the head of the household, and spread over the needs of a family, it was hardly adequate even for subsistence.

So it was that, in the footsteps of the giant of Idleness, the ogre of Want returned to Britain during the 1970s. By the end of the decade, according to the estimate of Frank Field, some seven million people – constituting more than one in eight of Britain's total population – lived below or close to the poverty line.

The politics of the liberal consensus, which had presided over a generation of economic and social progress during the 1950s and 1960s, had no answer to poverty and unemployment, or to the social tensions they caused. Their impotence in the face of the problems of the 1970s led to their eclipse by the end of the decade.

Whatever their nominal party affiliations, liberals shared the belief that the social and economic framework of Britain was fundamentally sound; and all that was required to make it work effectively were changes in the procedures by which decision-making in Britain was carried out.

They focused their attention particularly on the procedures of collective bargaining in the labour market. The liberal governments of the 1964–79 period attempted to deal with the rigidities they perceived in the labour market by reforming the legislative framework of industrial relations, and by introducing the new instrument of incomes policy to tackle wage inflation.

Both industrial relations reform, and incomes policy, have demonstrably failed. The record shows that they have neither reduced the incidence of strikes nor eliminated wage inflation. Both accelerated during the 1970s. During the years 1946 to 1968, the number of working days lost through strikes only rose above 3·5m. in the two years 1957 and 1962; while since 1968, working days lost through strikes have been consistently higher than 3·5m. a year, averaging 11·2m. in the fourteen years 1968–81; and they reached successive peaks at precisely the times when governments were seeking to intervene most actively in the labour market. The first such peak coincided with the battle over "In Place of Strife" in 1969; the second peak with the struggle over the Industrial Relations Act in 1972; and the third with the Winter of Discontent which followed the collapse of the Callaghan Government's incomes policy in 1978–79.

Government intervention in the labour market made worse the very problems with which it purported to deal. It forced organised labour to wage a defensive struggle to protect its historic rights and to preserve the ability of trade unions to act as effective bargaining agents for their members.

Even if the governments of the 1964–79 period had been successful in weakening the power of organised labour through legal reform, and in regulating the outcome of the collective bargaining process through incomes policy, their success would have made no positive contribution to resolving the underlying problems of the British economy. The labour market has not been the source of these problems; like the market for consumer goods, the market for labour responds to impulses elsewhere in the economy, rather than itself being an independent source of impulses. In particular, inflation in post-war Britain has not arisen as a result of aggressive upward pressure on wages, but rather because the growth of monetary demand has outstripped the capacity of the economy to produce goods to absorb that demand.

The attempt of the liberal consensus to deal with the problems it faced by means of institutional reform met with no greater success in Northern Ireland than it had in the labour market. The introduction of a system of proportional representation ended in failure after the strike of the Ulster Workers' Council of May 1974, which brought down the power-sharing executive. After that, the British Government was forced back to direct rule of Northern Ireland from Westminster, a response which solved none of the fundamental problems, and was seen on all sides as merely a second-best, makeshift solution.

The institutional reform bringing about British membership of the European Economic Community was heralded as a triumph for "moderation" against the extremes of left and right; but the promised benefits of entry had not been realised by the end of the 1970s. In narrow financial terms, Britain was by 1980 the largest net contributor to the Community's budget, although she had a lower real income per head than most of the other members. The financial costs could have been justified if the broader economic benefits of Community membership for which its advocates had hoped had been realised. But here again, the belief that institutional reform would eliminate the rigidities of the British economy and enable it to take advantage of new trading opportunities proved unfounded.

The two institutional reforms in the British parliamentary system advocated by the British Liberal Party met with equally little success. These reforms were the devolution of government, and the proposal to alter the system of election from first-past-the-post to proportional representation. Devolution gained insufficient electoral support at a referendum held on the issue in Scotland and Wales in March 1979; while the concept of proportional representation was rejected by the two major parties because the first-past-the-post system had a built-in bias in their favour and against any third party.

Thus, each of the major reforms promoted by liberals during the 1970s either ended in failure or was never implemented.

Liberalism failed because its most basic assumption about the causes of Britain's problems was wrong. The liberals believed that if only the flaws in the institutions through which Britain was governed were eradicated, then the economic problems of inflation, rising unemployment, and slow growth could be overcome. In fact, the relationship was the exact opposite: only if Britain's economic problems were overcome, and the economy set on a path of self-sustaining growth, could attempts at institutional reform have any chance of success.

The fundamental cause of Britain's problems since the late 1960s has been the absence of economic growth. Superimposed upon this has been a multitude of other factors: religious conflict in Northern Ireland; racial tensions in the decaying urban areas which used to be the heartland of Britain's industrial prosperity; and class conflict exacerbated by government's misguided attempts at intervention in the labour market.

The reversal of Britain's economic decline will not of itself solve these religious, social and political problems; but it is a necessary condition for them to be solved. A growing economy will at least engender an atmosphere of hope, and encourage different groups to work together for their common benefit, which is just not possible in a declining economy where everyone is struggling to protect their own interests first.

The New Orthodoxy of monetarism has done nothing to engender an atmosphere of hope; quite the reverse. It too has failed, like the old liberal consensus, because its analysis of Britain's problems is seriously flawed. The monetarist hypothesis is that inflation in the post-war world has been primarily caused by excessive growth of monetary demand; and that the solution to inflation therefore lies in reining back the growth of the money supply to the level that can be sustained by real output.

The particular method of reducing monetary growth adopted by the New Orthodoxy entailed curbing public spending, and checking the growth of private sector credit by allowing the rate of interest to rise. This strategy has brought down inflation only at the cost of a sharp contraction in Britain's productive base, especially in the manufacturing sector, which means that the economy is in much worse shape to take advantage of any upturn in world trade than it was when the Thatcher Government took office.

The problems caused by the New Orthodoxy derive from the errors in its assumptions.

Its first assumption is that inflation in the United Kingdom has been principally caused by monetary growth. As has been emphasised, inflation is a condition which occurs when monetary demand outstrips the capacity of the economy to produce goods to meet that demand; and inflation in the U.K. has been higher than in the western world as a whole, not because money supply has grown more rapidly in Britain than elsewhere (in fact, monetary growth in Britain has been slower than in the industrialised world as a whole since 1950), but rather because Britain's productive capacity has not grown as fast. So if Britain's inflationary problem is to be resolved, the first objective should be to increase the productive capacity of the economy.

The second assumption of the Orthodoxy is that the main culprit of high monetary growth has been public sector borrowing, and hence attempts at monetary restraint must focus first on restraint in the public sector. In point of fact, the contribution of the public sector to monetary growth has been much less important than the contribution of the private sector since 1970.

The third assumption is that the growth of private sector credit can be curbed by allowing interest rates to rise, without resort to direct controls. In fact, there is little evidence that the private sector's demand for credit is particularly sensitive to the rate of interest – bank lending to the private sector showed its most rapid growth in 1972–73 and in 1978–81, both of which were periods of high and rising interest rates. This suggests that the causal relationship has run from the demand for credit to the rate of interest, which is the price of credit – and not the other way about.

The fourth assumption is that the public sector is in competition with the private sector for resources. This may be true in certain circumstances, but it is by no means a universal truth. More often, the public and private sectors are complementary, with the public sector providing social and economic infrastructure like schools, hospitals, and the transport, telecommunications, and energy networks, which are necessary for the efficient working of the private sector.

The erroneous assumptions of the New Orthodoxy had led it to adopt policies which have had a disastrous effect on the real economy. In the public sector, efforts to retrench have fallen hardest on investment, which has undermined the productive base of the economy, and thus caused a rise in unemployment which has put further pressure on government's recurrent spending. In the private sector, the regime of high interest rates and demand deflation has also hit investment harder than consumption, and caused cutbacks and job losses.

By sacrificing the real economy to the chimerical pursuit of "sound money", the New Orthodoxy was repeating the tragic errors of the inter-war Treasury Orthodoxy, and setting in train a vicious circle of falling real national income, rising unemployment and, associated with it, greater poverty and social deprivation.

II

There may be a feeling that this book has been too unremittingly critical of the course of economic policy-making in Britain since the mid-1960s. But it is honestly difficult to think of one solitary area of economic policy over this period that can be accounted a success.

At various times, governments have had as objectives high employment, low inflation, wage increases linked to productivity growth, a surplus on the Balance of Payments, and a strong currency. Not one of these objectives has been realised for a prolonged period. Unemployment has risen to levels not seen since the depths of the Great Depression half a century ago. Inflation accelerated during the 1970s and, even in the early 1980s, despite a savage deflation, it remained higher than in the 1950s and 1960s. Money wages accelerated alongside prices, and this acceleration bore no relation whatever to productivity growth. And the British currency steadily depreciated against every one of the world's major trading currencies, reflecting the chronic weakness of Britain's Balance of Payments; a weakness arrested only temporarily and fortuitously by the exploitation of North Sea Oil.

The story has been one of total and unrelieved failure.

It could all be so different. If the leaders of Britain could escape from the murky fog in which they have been engulfed during the Age of Illusions, and see clearly what is important and what is peripheral in the management of the economy, then they could liberate those whose daily lives are bounded by the humiliation of the dole-queue; the tedium of enforced idleness; the continual struggle for survival on a subsistence income; the frustration of being unable to build a home or provide adequately for a family.

The principal goal of economic policy should be, quite simply, economic growth. The government could almost forget about all the other targets; because high employment, low inflation, and a strong trading position, will all flow naturally from a growth economy, as they have in West Germany and Japan.

Economic policy should be targeted towards the attainment of a steady growth rate of at least five per cent a year in real terms. Anything lower would be insufficient to make significant inroads into unemployment. In order to achieve this growth rate, the aggregate level of investment must be increased, and its quality improved. The instruments of economic policy should be designed to achieve this.

Monetary policy should not rely solely, or even mainly, on changes in the interest rate to regulate monetary growth. The rate of interest has not proved effective as a means of restricting the growth of private credit, because the knowledge borrowers have about the exact cost of their credit is imperfect, and in any event their decisions as to how much to borrow are influenced less by the cost of borrowing than by the return or utility they expect to derive from purchases made with borrowed money, and the ease with which they can borrow. So if the government wishes to choke off the growth of private credit, it is not enough to make it more expensive: the availability of credit must be restricted. This in turn implies that the old Keynesian tools of direct regulations and credit controls should be resuscitated. Such controls can be used to curb consumer borrowing, by restricting the availability of credit cards and hire purchase facilities. On the other hand, borrowing for investment would be left untouched. There is some evidence that high interest rates have the opposite effect: their maximum effect is on borrowing for investment, while borrowing for consumption purposes is left largely unaffected.

In order to establish precisely what are the effects of monetary policy, the information base needs to be developed. In particular, statistics for both public sector borrowing and bank lending to the private sector should distinguish between the components for consumption and for investment. Consumer borrowing needs to be tightly regulated; while borrowing for investment should be positively encouraged in times of high unemployment because, over time, it will result in the creation of additional job opportunities.

To the extent that government wishes to control the aggregate supply of money, the best method would appear to be through the control of the monetary base, rather than trying to influence some broadly-defined monetary total. Recent history has shown that such totals are easy for the banking system to manipulate.

Complementary with the reforms in monetary policy, greater attention should be given to *fiscal policy* – government's policy with reference to its own revenue and expenditure.

On the revenue side, it is necessary to go back to first principles. Ideally, a tax system should be as simple as possible to administer; efficient, in the sense that it raises the required revenues at least cost; difficult to evade; equitable, falling most heavily on those best able to pay; and finally, it should not encourage consumption at the expense of investment.

The efforts over the years of a plethora of politicians, civil servants, and their advisers, have resulted in a tax system which contravenes not one, but all of these basic criteria. The maze of reliefs, rebates, allowances, and exemptions, is intelligible only to a small cadre of highly trained lawyers, accountants, and tax experts, who are invariably the most highly paid, often the most able – and unquestionably the most socially useless members of their professions. If their talents are to be put to better use, it is imperative that the U.K. tax system is given a radical overhaul.

This overhaul should entail the following reforms.

Firstly, reliefs for the payment of interest on mortgages, which cost the Exchequer an estimated £2,150m. in the 1982–83 financial year, should be phased out. Not only is this relief highly inequitable, but it has failed to provide a stimulus for the construction of more and better homes, and become instead a mechanism for inflating house prices. The rising price of houses has generated unearned inflationary gains for householders, which have served to undermine the incentive to invest in productive enterprise. The proportion of personal wealth held in property in the U.K. was one-third by 1980, a higher proportion than in any other major economy. This was an important reason for the lower rate of industrial investment in Britain than among her major competitors.

Politically, the phasing out of mortgage relief would be unpopular, which is why the system still exists. But if the relief was phased out during a period of falling interest rates, then the transitional phase would be relatively painless. The extra cost a taxpayer would incur as a consequence of the phasing out of the relief would be offset by the lower interest payable on his mortgage, so that he would be no worse off overall.

The second reform would entail the reduction of the allowances available for contributions towards pensions and life insurance. Like mortgage interest relief, these allowances are inequitable, because they can be set against the highest marginal slice of income. The allowances exist because government wishes to encourage individuals to save for their old age, which in principle is laudable. But the nature of the allowances, which are available only for payments into approved pension and life assurance schemes, and not for saving in general, has caused a concentration of finance capital in the hands of a few institutions. The institutions, by their very nature as trustees of other people's money, are cautious and risk-averse investors, who have not achieved a particularly good return on their investments. The tax breaks available for payments into pension and life assurance funds have thus seriously distorted the flow of investable funds in the economy.

To correct the imbalance, the allowances should be reduced, so that contributions into approved schemes can be offset only to the extent of between 5 and 10 per cent of the taxpayer's income, rather than $16\frac{2}{3}$ per cent in the case of life assurance relief, and $17\frac{1}{2}$ per cent in the case of pension contributions, as during the 1982–83 fiscal year. In addition, to make the system more equitable, the allowances should be given only against the basic rate of income tax. The greater tax-base this would generate for the Exchequer could be matched by an increase in the tax threshold (the single person's allowance), combined with higher State pensions for the elderly. An increase in the basic State pension would ensure that all the elderly have an adequate income on which to live, and not merely a proportion fortunate enough to have been employed on a salary sufficient to pay into private pension schemes.

The third reform proposed is the ending of the married man's allowance. Apart from any other considerations, it is inconsistent with the provisions of Equal Opportunities legislation, in that it is blatantly discriminatory against women. Nor does it help the families most in need: since they are mostly families where the main breadwinner either is a woman, or is unemployed, and in neither case eligible for the married man's allowance. Since families on low incomes with children to support make up a large proportion of those living close to the povery line, it is important that a government concerned with ending poverty should give them help. But there are far more effective means of achieving this than the married man's allowance – notably child benefits, combined with a mother's allowance paid to women (or to men without wives) who have dependent children. As Frank Field has pointed out, "The achievement of a generous system of child benefits, together with the beginnings of a mother's allowance, would not only eradicate family poverty as we know it today, but would also increase in a very real sense the economic freedom of many households with children." (*Inequality in Britain: Freedom, Welfare and the State*, p. 184.)

In sum, what is proposed are substantial cuts in reliefs and allowances, combined with an increase in the tax threshold, and the payment of taxable cash benefits to individuals whom the State wishes to help. The switch from personal tax allowances to cash benefits would greatly ameliorate the problem of Want in Britain. Allowances cannot benefit those whose incomes are too low to absorb them, which includes all of the unemployed; and they give the greatest benefits to those with the highest incomes, who need them least. Cash benefits would have the opposite effect on income distribution, and would be a far more effective means of combating poverty than the national insurance system; because cash benefits would be paid on the basis of need, whereas an insurance scheme remunerates people only on the basis of their former means, as measured by what they have contributed to it.

The reforms to simplify and rationalise the system of personal income taxation should be complemented by reforms in the tax treatment of corporate income. Stock relief, an emergency measure introduced during a period of high price inflation combined with falling real remand in the mid-1970s, should be phased out. The complex rules for the taxation of a company in its opening and closing years should be simplified. The system of capital allowances should also be reviewed. The overall objective should be to broaden the tax base, and correspondingly lower the rate of company tax, so that corporate decision-making is not distorted by an unnecessarily cumbersome tax environment.

On the expenditure side, government should give incentives to investment in the small enterprise sector, where there has been a funding gap. The government should seek to extend and place on a permanent basis the small business loan guarantee scheme. The tax incentives introduced in 1980 and 1981 to encourage individuals to buy shares in newly-formed private companies should also be maintained. The funds available to the Co-operative Development Agency should be increased to enable it to expand the technical advice and finance with which it can assist co-operative enterprises. Consideration should also be given to the establishment of a Small Firms Investment Company, along the lines proposed by a minority of the Wilson Committee on financial institutions, which would be funded in part out of the government's revenues from North Sea Oil.

However, even with a more favourable fiscal environment, it is unlikely that investment in the private sector will grow at a rate sufficient to generate full employment. The industrialised world is currently in the downswing of the long Kondratieff wave, so that private investment is likely to grow only sluggishly under its own steam.

The public sector must itself become an engine for growth, through its *capital investment policy*. The size of the investment programme should be determined by the target rate of growth, and the contribution of the private sector towards achieving that target. As ball-park figures, the real rate of economic growth must be not less than 5 per cent a year if significant inroads are to be made into unemployment; and the real level of investment should grow by a minimum of 10 per cent a year to achieve this. In the early stages of recovery, the growth of investment should be more like 15 per cent a year in order to pull the economy out of the slump.

Gross domestic fixed capital formation in 1980 and 1981 was just under £40 billion, so 15 per cent real growth, after allowing for inflation, would require an increase in the monetary value of investment in the region of £8 billion–£11 billion, in 1981 prices. Projections should be made of the amount by which private sector investment is likely to increase; on past trends, depending on the phase of the trade cycle, it could be as much as £3 billion or as little as zero. This would leave government's capital works programme needing to grow by between £5 billion and £11 billion per annum.

Once the overall targets are laid down, the government should assess which particular investment projects should come on stream to meet them. The projects implemented might include schemes to upgrade the transport and communications infrastructure, such as the Channel Tunnel and the electrification of the railways; projects to increase the production of energy from renewable natural resources, such as the Severn Barrage; and assistance to innovatory investment in high technology through a revived National Enterprise Board.

In addition to the development of economic infrastructure, the government should allocate funds to upgrading the nation's social infrastructure: its housing, hospitals, schools, water and sewage. Some of the additional revenues raised by phasing out mortage interest relief could be used to actually build more houses and to redevelop the blighted inner areas of Britain's major cities.

The funding of the investment programme would be largely through debt, at least in the early stages of recovery. Government should aim at a surplus on its current account, and use this surplus as its equity contribution to its capital projects. However, initially it is unlikely that the government's current surplus will be very great, if indeed it is achieved at all, because government has to carry a heavy burden of unemployed on a tax base that has been reduced by the decline of the real economy.

So most of the programme will have to be financed by debt. The most suitable form of debt would not be short-term Treasury Bills, but rather long-term bonds, linked to specified projects and not necessarily wholly government-guaranteed. The private sector would thus carry some of the risks for projects which would ultimately benefit it. For example, a Channel Tunnel Bond could be issued to assist in the financing of the Channel Tunnel, with a 50 per cent government guarantee, so that if the project did not prove viable the investor would stand to lose up to half of his investment. To make this worthwhile, the investor would be offered a fixed rate of interest, plus a right to participate in the profits of the venture, plus the right to vote for half of the Board of Directors (with the remainder being nominated by government)

Ideally, an investment-led reflation in Britain would be matched by a reflation elsewhere among her major trading partners, particularly within the European Economic Community. If there was a co-ordinated reflation, then there could be a virtuous circle of mutually growing trade, so that each country would balance its international payments and receipts at a higher volume.

If there were no co-ordinated reflation, then Britain would run the risk of facing the same problems as President Mitterrand's France. In 1981–82, France experienced slight real growth while the United States, West Germany and Britain all declined; and as a direct result, France drew in more imports, while her exports failed to grow, and consequently she ran into Balance of Payments difficulties.

In the absence of a co-ordinated reflation in Britain, it may prove necessary to supplement an investment-led reflation with a degree of protection for domestic industry. However, not too much faith should be placed in protection: France's introduction of protective measures has not enabled her to reflate, freed from Balance of Payments constraints. Nevertheless, a temporary imposition of tariffs might provide a wall behind which British industry could rebuild. It might also be acceptable to Britain's trading partners, if such a protective wall resulted in a higher level of economic activity and thus enabled Britain to purchase a greater volume of imports in the medium term.

Overall, the economic strategy would be directed towards the pursuit of economic growth through investment. Monetary policy would be designed to restrict the growth of consumer credit, and to keep the rate of interest as low as possible so that the cost of borrowing for investment is cheap. Fiscal policy would be changed to end the discrimination against industrial investment, and would be structured positively to encourage it. And the public sector's own capital investment policy would act as the major engine of growth in the economy, and absorb any idle funds in the money markets by the development of new debt instruments appropriate for the financing of specific projects. It might also be necessary to revise trade policy to help ensure that the additional demand generated by the growth of investment feeds through to output and employment within Britain, and is not sucked out of the economy in extra spending on imports.

The whole strategy would thus cohere, and the instruments of economic policy would work in harness, driving towards the creation of additional productive capacity and employment in a non-inflationary way. The failures of the Age of Illusions would not be overcome overnight, but once the initial major push was given, the economy could be set on a path of self-sustaining growth which would make full employment attainable by the end of the 1980s.

The alternative to a strategy such as this is Britain's continued economic decline; and the potential social consequences of this are already becoming clear.

In the 1930s it took the shock of war and the threat of imminent destruction to jolt the British ruling classes out of their complacency and force them to re-examine the ideas which they had accepted as axiomatic.

It may take a comparable shock to jolt Britain's contemporary rulers, and force them to re-think their most fundamental beliefs. And such a shock may come, not from outside as during the 1930s, but from within, from the crumbling of Britain's social fabric.

During the summer of 1981, sporadic rioting and looting spread through Britain's major cities. These were the areas, in Liverpool, Manchester, and London, where urban decay was worst; where the level of unemployment was highest; the standard of housing and the quality of social amenities lowest; and where there seemed least hope for improvement within the existing framework of society.

Social unrest will only be overcome when Britain is once more moving forward, and the economy is growing and offering opportunities for its people to fulfil their most basic aspirations for decent homes, secure jobs, and a stable future.

If the country continues to decline, social unrest may get worse, and the government may react by adopting authoritarian measures in an effort to suppress it. In this case, the British mainland will be treading the dangerous path of Northern Ireland in the early 1970s;

and the United Kingdom may experience during the 1980s misery on a scale unparalleled even in the inter-war years.

But there is yet a chance that the 1980s will be, not a decade of violence, waste, and repression, but rather a decade of hope and progress. If Britain's political leaders have the vision to give paramount emphasis to the need for economic growth; the competence to design a strategy to achieve it; and the determination to push that strategy through; then it is possible that the 1980s will be the decade when Britain rises again like a phoenix from the ashes, to inspire a new optimism within the country, and renewed respect from the world outside, as her people, of all races and religions, start to work and build together for their common good.

This is the challenge of the 1980s.

STATISTICAL APPENDICES

Sources of the Tables which follow, and from which figures for the Tables and Graphs in the text have been obtained:

Table I: Labour Market Indicators
Figures for the years to 1966 are derived from L.C.E.S. **The British Economy, Key Statistics, 1900–1966* (London, Times Newspapers). Figures for the post-1966 period are derived from various editions of the *Annual Abstract of Statistics*. Strike statistics are derived from the *Employment & Productivity Gazette*.

Table II: Money and Prices
II(a). International data is derived from the I.M.F. Survey of November 12th, 1979, and updated by the December 1982 edition of the I.M.F.'s *International Financial Statistics*. The rate of change of the U.K. cost-of-living index is derived from L.C.E.S., *The British Economy, Key Statistics* for 1952–66, and from the *Annual Abstract of Statistics* for the years since 1966.
II(b). The figures for British monetary growth are derived from the *Bank of England Quarterly Bulletin* of 1969, pp. 372–82, for the years 1952–68; and various editions of the *Bank of England Quarterly Bulletin* (Tables 11.1–11.3) for post-1968 data.

Table III: Real investment, GDP, and Output
Figures derived from C.S.O., *Economic Trends: Annual Supplement, 1982 Edition*, Tables 14 (for national income figures) and 80 (for the indices of industrial and manufacturing production).

* London and Cambridge Economic Services.

I. Key Indicators of the British Labour Market since 1946

Year	*% rate of unemployment*	*% change in earnings over previous year*		*Strikes*	
		in money terms	*in real terms*	*'000 workers involved*	*Million working days lost*
1946	2·5	5·6	2·1	526	2·2
1947	3·1	6·8	1·4	620	2·4
1948	1·8	8·1	1·3	424	1·9
1949	1·6	4·2	1·2	433	1·8
1950	1·5	5·6	2·4	302	1·4
1951	1·2	10·1	0·9	379	1·7
1952	2·1	7·9	(1·1)	415	1·8
1953	1·8	6·2	3·0	1,370	2·2
1954	1·5	6·5	4·7	448	2·5
1955	1·2	9·3	4·8	659	3·8
1956	1·3	8·0	3·0	507	2·1
1957	1·6	4·7	1·0	1,356	8·4
1958	2·2	3·4	0·5	523	3·5
1959	2·3	4·5	4·0	645	5·3
1960	1·7	6·5	5·4	817	3·0
1961	1·6	6·1	2·7	771	3·0
1962	2·1	3·5	(0·7)	4,420	5·8
1963	2·6	4·2	2·2	591	2·0
1964	1·7	8·6	5·3	873	2·3
1965	1·5	8·0	3·2	868	2·9
1966	1·6	5·8	1·9	530	2·4
1967	2·3	3·9	1·5	731	2·8
1968	2·5	8·2	3·5	2,255	4·7
1969	2·5	7·8	2·4	1,654	6·8
1970	2·6	12·0	5·6	1,793	11·0
1971	3·5	11·3	1·9	1,171	13·6
1972	3·9	12·9	5·8	1,722	23·9
1973	2·7	13·2	4·0	1,513	7·2
1974	2·6	17·7	(11·0)	1,622	14·7
1975	4·2	26·7	2·5	789	6·0
1976	5·7	15·7	(0·8)	666	3·3
1977	6·2	10·1	(5·7)	1,155	10·1
1978	6·1	14·4	6·1	1,001	9·4
1979	5·7	15·6	2·2	4,583	29·5
1980	7·4	20·6	2·6	830	12·0
1981	11·3	12·9	1·0	1,499	4·3

II(a). Money and Prices since 1952

Year	*Internationally % change in 12 months in:* world consumer prices*	primary commodity prices†	world money supply	*The U.K. % change in 12 months in:* retail prices	money supply (Sterling M3)
1952	3·9		5·3	9·1	2·8
1953	1.5		4·3	3·2	3·1
1954	1·1		6·5	1·8	3·0
1955	1·3		5·7	4·5	−2·7
1956	3·0		4·7	5·0	0·9
1957	3·9			3·7	3·1
1958	4·2	−8·9	4·7	2·9	3·0
1959	3·3	−1·4	7·0	0·5	6·1
1960	2·9	−0·1	5·0	1·1	1·8
1961	2·6	−4·0	6·8	3·4	2·5
1962	3·6	−1·8	7·0	4·2	2·6
1963	4·1	6·1	9·1	2·0	6·5
1964	4·6	6·9	9·7	3·3	5·2
1965	4·9	−1·9	8·5	4·8	7·6
1966	5·1	3·1	7·6	3·9	3·4
1967	4·2	−6·3	7·0	2·4	9·3
1968	4·4	−0·8	9·1	4·7	7·3
1969	5·2	8·0	8·7	5·4	2·4
1970	6·0	3·7	7·6	6·4	9·5
1971	5·9	−5·8	11·9	9·4	13·8
1972	5·8	13·9	13·4	7·1	26·5
1973	9·6	54·2	13·9	9·2	26·0
1974	15·3	27·6	11·6	28·7	10·2
1975	13·4	−17·7	12·8	24·2	6·5
1976	11·1	12·3	15·1	16·5	9·5
1977	11·4	20·4	13·1	15·8	10·0
1978	9·7	−4·7	14·2	8·3	14·9
1979	12·1	12·4	13·4	13·4	12·7
1980	15·4	9·7	11·5	18·6	18·5
1981	13·7	−14·7	10·8	11·9	13·2

* The I.M.F. Survey comments on its derivation of the rate of change of world prices that "the Fund's monthly publication, *International Financial Statistics* [I.F.S.] provides current monthly averages of country consumer price indices . . . derived from the consumer price indices of 115 countries (they exclude Albania, Bulgaria, the People's Republic of China, Cuba, Czechoslovakia, the German Democratic Republic, Hungary, Mongolia, North Korea, Poland, and the U.S.S.R.). The I.F.S. calculations therefore provide current monthly calculations covering most of the world." (I.M.F. Survey, November 12th, 1979, p. 353.) The Fund has pointed out to the author, however, that membership included both Hungary and the People's Republic of China as of May 1983, and that the number of reporting countries has increased considerably since 1979.

† The I.M.F. Survey comments that "these changes should be interpreted with particular caution, because of the limitations of the component measures from which they are estimated".

II(b). Monetary Growth in the U.K. since 1952 (£m.)

Year	Public Sector Borrowing Requirement (P.S.B.R.) −	Sales of public sector debt to non-bank private sector =	Net contribution of public sector to D.C.E. +	Net changes in bank lending to overseas and private sectors =	Domestic Credit Expansion (D.C.E.) +	Change in foreign exchange and net non-deposit liabilities =	Growth of money supply Sterling M3	Money Supply Sterling M3, at Jan. 1st	% rate of growth of Sterling M3 per year
1952	771	269	502	−451	51	184	235	8,649	2·7
1953	591	285	306	−13	293	−26	267	8,884	3·0
1954	367	293	74	268	342	−74	268	9,151	2·9
1955	469	699	−230	138	−92	−156	−248	9,419	−2·6
1956	564	562	2	73	75	6	81	9,171	0·9
1957	486	320	166	35	201	27	228	9,252	2·5
1958	491	807	−316	419	103	171	274	9,480	2·9
1959	571	768	−197	943	746	−168	578	9,754	5·9
1960	710	1,082	−372	757	385	−203	182	10,332	1·8
1961	704	510	194	319	513	−251	262	10,514	2·5
1962	546	831	−285	560	275	—	275	10,776	2·6
1963	824	575	249	798	1,047	−350	697	11,051	6·3
1964	989	504	485	1,023	1,508	−855	653	11,748	5·6
1965	1,205	488	717	395	1,112	−185	927	12,401	7·5
1966	963	262	701	12	713	−267	446	13,328	3·3
1967	1,863	665	1,198	536	1,734	−482	1,252	13,774	9·1
1968	1,291	−11	1,302	677	1,979	−963	1,016	15,026	6·8
1969	−449	354	−803	577	−226	600	374	16,042	2·3
1970	−10	102	−112	854	742	799	1,541	16,416	9·4

1971	1,364	2,110	−746	1,923	1,177	1,282	2,459	17,957	13·7
1972	2,055	1,010	1,045	5,646	6,691	−1,764	4,927	20,416	24·1
1973	4,200	2,295	1,905	6,161	8,066	−1,364	6,702	25,343	26·4
1974	6,370	3,168	3,202	3,724	6,926	−3,671	3,255	32,045	10·2
1975	10,501	5,571	4,930	−399	4,531	−2,200	2,331	35,300	6·6
1976	9,198	5,770	3,428	4,054	7,482	−3,917	3,565	37,631	9·5
1977	5,993	8,456	−2,463	3,593	1,130	3,000	4,130	41,196	10·0
1978	8,357	6,021	2,336	5,760	8,096	−1,324	6,772	45,326	14·9
1979	12,608	10,885	1,723	8,574	10,297	−3,682	6,615	52,098	12·7
1980	12,189	9,435	2,754	12,828	15,582	−4,668	10,914	58,713	18·6
1981	10,582	11,132	−550	14,596	14,046	−4,637	9,409	69,627	13·5
1982	5,428	10,422	−4,994	21,718	16,724	−8,654	8,070	79,036	10.2

III. The Growth of Investment, Income and Output in the U.K. since 1948 (in constant 1975 terms)

	£ million, 1975 prices			INDICES OF INDUSTRIAL PRODUCTION *Seasonally adjusted Average 1975=100*		
Year	*Gross domestic product At market prices*	*Gross domestic fixed capital formation*	*GDFCF as a % of GDP*	*All industries covered*	*Manufac-turing*	*Year*
1948	51,029	6,082	11·9	50·3	46·9	1948
1949	52,546	6,645	12·6	53·5	50·3	1949
1950	54,193	7,025	13·0	56·7	54·1	1950
1951	56,163	7,074	12·6	58·1	55·7	1951
1952	56,027	7,123	12·7	56·3	53·0	1952
1953	58,607	7,908	13·5	59·9	56·8	1953
1954	60,849	8,597	14·1	62·9	59·8	1954
1955	63,182	9,106	14·4	66·0	63·6	1955
1956	64,241	9,536	14·8	66·5	63·4	1956
1957	65,487	10,058	15·4	67·8	64·9	1957
1958	65,541	10,142	15·5	67·2	64·4	1958
1959	68,131	10,918	16·0	70·6	68·1	1959
1960	71,326	11,905	16·7	75·4	73·5	1960
1961	73,713	13,070	17·7	76·4	73·7	1961
1962	74,340	13,096	17·6	77·1	73·9	1962
1963	77,358	13,269	17·1	79·3	76·5	1963
1964	81,447	15,494	19·0	86·1	83·4	1964
1965	83,372	16,240	19·5	88·7	85·8	1965
1966	85,095	16,643	19·6	90·1	87·4	1966
1967	87,338	18,052	20·7	91·1	87·9	1967
1968	90,965	18,878	20·8	96·9	94·1	1968
1969	92,270	18,954	20·5	99·5	97·7	1969
1970	94,345	19,460	20·6	99·6	98·1	1970
1971	96,912	19,743	20·4	99·7	97·5	1971
1972	99,111	19,823	20·0	101·9	100·1	1972
1973	106,553	21,195	19·9	109·4	108·4	1973
1974	105,481	20,567	19·5	105·1	106·6	1974
1975	104,907	20,416	19·5	100·0	100·0	1975
1976	108,734	20,649	19·0	102·0	101·4	1976
1977	110,114	20,161	18·3	105·9	102·9	1977
1978	113,764	20,836	18·3	109·8	103·9	1978
1979	115,355	20,898	18·1	112·6	104·4	1979
1980	113,793	20,761	18·2	105·1	95·1	1980
1981	111,393	18,774	16·9	100·4	89·4	1981

SELECT BIBLIOGRAPHY

Andrzewjewski, Stanislaw: *Military Organisation and Society*, Routledge & Kegan Paul, 1954.

Atkinson, A. B.: *The Economics of Inequality*, Oxford, Clarendon Press, 1975.

Bacon, Robert, and Eltis, Walter: *Britain's Economic Problem: Too Few Producers*, Macmillan, 1976.

Beckerman, Wilfred (ed.): *The Labour Government's Economic Record, 1964–1970*, Duckworth, 1972.

Beveridge, W. H.: *Report on Social Insurance and Allied Services* (2 vols), H.M.S.O., 1942.

Beveridge, W. H.: *Full Employment in a Free Society*, Allen & Unwin, 1944.

Butler, R.A.: *The Art of the Possible*, Hamish Hamilton, 1971.

Cairncross, Sir Alec (ed.): *Britain's Economic Prospects Reconsidered*, Allen & Unwin, 1970.

Caves, Richard (ed.): *Britain's Economic Prospects*, Allen & Unwin, 1968.

Clegg, H. A.: *How to run an Incomes Policy and why we made such a Mess of the Last One*, Heinemann, 1971.

Clemence, R. V. (ed.): *The Essays of J. A. Schumpeter*, Addison-Wesley (Cambridge, Mass.), 1951.

Corden, W. M.: *The Theory of Protection*, Oxford University Press, 1971.

Corden, W. M,: *Trade Policy and Economic Welfare*, Oxford University Press, 1974.

Cramp, A. B.: *Monetary Management: Principles and Practice*, Allen & Unwin, 1971.

Crosland, C. A. R.: *The Future of Socialism*, Cape, 1956.

Crosland, Susan, *Tony Crosland*, Cape, 1982.

Crossman, Richard: *Diaries of a Cabinet Minister* (3 vols), Hamilton and Cape, 1975–77.

Donovan Commission: *Report on Trade Unions and Employers' Associations, 1965–1968*, H.M.S.O., 1968.

Feinstein, C. H.: *National Income, Expenditure and Output in the United Kingdom, 1855–1965*, Cambridge University Press, 1972.

Field, Frank: *Inequality in Britain: Freedom, Welfare and the State*, Fontana, 1981.

Foot, Michael: *Aneurin Bevan*, Vol. I, MacGibbon & Kee, 1962, Vol. II, Davis-Poynter, 1973.

Fraser, Derek: *The Evolution of the Welfare State: A history of social policy since the industrial revolution*, Macmillan, 1973.

Friedman, Milton: "The Role of Monetary Policy", *American Economic Review*, 1968.

Friedman, Milton: *The Optimum Quantity of Money and Other Essays*, Macmillan, 1969.

Halsey, A. H. (ed.): *Trends in British Society since 1900: A guide to the changing social structure of Britain*, Macmillan, 1972.

Hancock, W. K., and Gowing, M.: *The British War Economy*, H.M.S.O., 1949.

Hiro, Dilip: *Black British, White British*, Eyre & Spottiswoode, 1971.

Howson, Susan: *Domestic Monetary Management in Britain, 1919–1938*, Cambridge University Press, 1975.

Jackson, D., Turner, H. A., and Wilkinson, F.: *Do Trade Unions Cause Inflation?*, Cambridge University Press, 1972.

Jenkins, Peter: *The Battle of Downing Street*, Charles Knight, 1970.

Jones, Aubrey: *The New Inflation: The politics of prices and incomes*, André Deutsch, 1973.

Junz, H B., and Rhomberg, R. R.: "Price Competitiveness in Export Trade among Industrial Countries", *American Economic Review*, 1973.

Keynes, J. M.: *The Means to Prosperity*, Times Newspapers, London, 1933.

Keynes, J. M.: *The General Theory of Employment, Interest, and Money*, Macmillan, 1936.

Keynes, J. M.: "The General Theory of Employment", *Quarterly Journal of Economics*, 1937.

Keynes, J. M.: *How to Pay for the War*, Macmillan, 1940.

Kondratieff, N.: "The Long Waves in Economic Life", *Review of Economic Statistics*, 1935.

Lapping, Brian: *The Labour Government, 1964–1970*, Penguin, 1970.

London and Cambridge Economic Services (L.C.E.S.): *The British Economy: Key Statistics, 1900–1970*, Times Newspapers, London, 1971.

Matthews, R. C.O.: *The Trade Cycle*, Cambridge University Press, 1959.

Matthews, R. C. O.: "Postwar Business Cycles in the United Kingdom", in M. Bronfenbrenner (ed.): *Is the Business Cycle Obsolete?*, Wiley-Interscience, 1969.

Matthews, R. C. O.: "Why has Britain had Full Employment since the War?" *Economic Journal*, 1968.

Mitchell, B. R., and Deane, P. M.: *Abstract of British Historical Statistics*, Cambridge University Press, 1962.

Mitchell, B. R., and Jones, H. G.: *Second Abstract of British Historical Statistics*, Cambridge University Press, 1971.

Moggridge, D. E.: *British Monetary Policy, 1924–1931*, Cambridge University Press, 1972.

Phillips, A. W.: "The Relation between Unemployment and the Rate of Change of Money Wage Rates in the United Kingdom, 1862–1957", *Economica*, 1958.

Pierce, D. G., and Shaw, D. M.: *Monetary Economics: Theories, Evidence and Policy*, Butterworths, 1974.

Pollard, Sidney: *The Development of the British Economy, 1914–1967*, Arnold, 1969.

Pollard, Sidney (ed.): *The Gold Standard and Employment Policies between the Wars*, Methuen, 1970.

Rau, N. K.: *Trade Cycles: Theory and Evidence*, Macmillan, 1974.

Rogow, A. A.: *The Labour Government and British Industry, 1945–1951*, Blackwell, Oxford, 1955.

Schumpeter, J. A.: *The Theory of Economic Development*, 1912, translated by Redvers Opie, Harvard University Press (Cambridge, Mass.), 1934; Oxford University Press (New York), 1961.

Schumpeter, J. A.: *Business Cycles* (2 vols), McGraw Hill, 1939.

Schumpeter, J. A.: *Capitalism, Socialism and Democracy*, 5th edn, Allen & Unwin, 1976.

Tew, Brian: "The Implementation of Monetary Policy in Post-War Britain", *Midland Bank Review*, Spring 1981.

Titmuss, R. M.: *Essays on the Welfare State*, Unwin University Books, 1958.

Trevithick, J. A., and Mulvey, C.: *The Economics of Inflation*, Martin Robertson, 1975.

Turner, H. A.: *Is Britain Really Strike Prone?* Cambridge University Press, 1969.

INDEX